DYLAN'S DAEMON LOVER:

The Tangled Tale of a 450-Year Old Pop Ballad.

by Clinton Heylin.

First edition published in April 1999 by Helter Skelter Publishing, in conjunction with Labour of Love Productions.

A CIP record for this book is available from the British Library.

ISBN 1-900924-15-3

Printed and bound in Great Britain by
Cromwell Press, Trowbridge, Wiltshire

Contents.

OTHER BOOKS BY THE AUTHOR:

- on Bob Dylan:

DYLAN BEHIND THE SHADES: THE BIOGRAPHY
DYLAN BEHIND CLOSED DOORS: THE RECORDING SESSIONS
DYLAN DAY BY DAY: A LIFE IN STOLEN MOMENTS

- on Popular Song:

RISE/FALL: A HISTORY OF PUBLIC IMAGE LIMITED
FORM AND SUBSTANCE: A HISTORY OF JOY DIVISION [with Craig
        Wood]
GYSPY LOVE SONGS & SAD REFRAINS: THE RECORDINGS OF
        RICHARD THOMPSON & SANDY DENNY.
FROM THE VELVETS TO THE VOIDOIDS: A PRE-PUNK HISTORY
BOOTLEG! [also published as THE GREAT WHITE WONDERS]
NEVER MIND THE BOLLOCKS, HERE'S THE SEX PISTOLS
THE PENGUIN BOOK OF ROCK & ROLL WRITING [editor]

forthcoming:
DYLAN BEHIND THE SHADES: A REVISIT [to be published May 2000]
CAN YOU FEEL THE SILENCE? Van Morrison: A Life In Music.

correspondence address:
maddog @ heylin.demon.co.uk

Preface - A Day in New York.

There's nobody that's going to kill traditional music. All these songs about roses growing out of people's brains and lovers who are really geese and swans that turn into angels - they're not going to die ... I listen to the old ballads ... I could give you a descriptive detail of what they do to me, but some people would probably think my imagination had gone mad ... [But] in that music is the only true, valid death you can feel today. - Bob Dylan, 1966.[1]

At approximately five o'clock on Wednesday, November 22, 1961, in a studio on the seventh floor of one of Columbia's Manhattan locales, a twenty-year old Robert Zimmerman was preparing to cut the last song at the sessions for his debut album, completed in two three-hour sessions, two days apart, under the guidance of Columbia's most experienced folk producer, the legendary John Hammond Snr.

Dylan had already recorded a broad cross-section of traditional American folk and blues songs, a Guthrie original, three of his own embryonic originals and even a heavily-Americanized rendition of a fine eighteenth century Scottish ballad, 'The Bonnie Lass o' Fyvie', now redubbed 'Pretty Peggy-O' (prefaced by Dylan, in his best Huck Finn voice, admitting that he has no idea where the song's site, Fenario, might be).

The young Dylan had just cut three songs in consecutive, single takes - 'Gospel Plow', 'Highway 51 Blues' and 'Freight Train Blues' - and was on a roll. But the song with which he wrapped up the sessions was not one he is known to have previously tackled (even in friends' living-rooms), nor is there another recording extant from his 'folk' days (Note: He would rerecord the song nine years later for the *Self Portrait* album. That version remains unreleased). It was a song from which there could be no immunity in folk circles, one of the common store of British ballads that also included 'Gypsy Davey', 'The Twa Sisters' and the ubiquitous

1

Dylan's Daemon Lover

'Barbara Allen' (all songs Dylan performed between 1960 and 1962). Prefacing this final cut with a spoken intro. - as already practised on 'You're No Good', 'Pretty Peggy-O' and 'Baby Let Me Follow You Down' - Dylan set up a driving guitar accompaniment to this extraordinary tale of unspoken vows, perfidy and supernatural retribution:

[spoken:] Here's a story about a ghost come back from out in the sea, come to take his bride away from the house carpenter.

1. Well met, well met, my own true love,
Well met, well met, cried he,
I've just returned from the salt, salt sea,
And it's all for the love of thee.

2. I could have married a king's daughter there,
She would have married me,
But I have forsaken my king's daughter there,
And it's all for the love of thee.

3. Well, if you could have married a king's daughter there,
I'm sure you're the one to blame,
For I am married to a house carpenter,
And I'm sure he's a fine young man.

4. Forsake, forsake your house carpenter,
And come away with me,
I'll take you to where the green grass grows,
On the shores of sunny Italy.

5. So up she picked her babies three,
And gave them kisses one-two-three, saying,
Take good care of your Daddy when I'm gone,
And keep him good company.

6. Well, they were sailing about two weeks,
I'm sure it was not three,
When the younger of the girls [sic], she came on deck,
Saying [she] wants company.

7. Well, are you weeping for your house and home,
Or are you weeping for your fee?
Well, I'm not weeping for my house carpenter,
I'm weeping for my babies three.

8. Oh what are those hills yonder, my love,
They look as white as snow,
Those are the hills of heaven, my love,
Where you and I'll never know.

9. What are those hills yonder, my love,
They look as black as night,
Those are the hills of hellfire, my love,
Where you and I will unite.

10. Oh, twice around went the gallant ship,
I'm sure it was not three,
When the ship all of a sudden sprung a leak
And drifted to the bottom of the sea.[2]

Most of Dylan's early traditional covers have an obvious source - the Clancys', 'Sing Out', other New York folkies, Alan Lomax's *Folksongs Of North America* &c. - but his source for 'The House Carpenter', the title by which the song has been popularly known in America for a century or more, is not so self-evident.

The 'Sing Out' version had been taken from a Richard Dyer-Bennet recording for Folkways, and is as far from Dylan's take aesthetically as it is lyrically. Harry Smith's much-lauded *Anthology Of American Folk Music*, which Greil Marcus has taken as the very font for Dylan's radical reconfiguration of folk, includes a 'House Carpenter' from a 1930 Columbia 78 by Clarence Ashley but, like the 'Love Henry' that precedes it on the *Anthology*, it is a quite different beast to the one Dylan committed to tape. Ashley has no hills of heaven or hell, nor shores of Italy. So much for the *Anthology*! Nor is Alan Lomax much help. The rendition in *Folksongs Of North America*, recorded from Texas Gladden and released on a Library of Congress LP in 1956, has a fine, fine tune but disjointed lyrics, neither of which have been appropriated by Dylan.

3

So are there any probable first-hand sources? He could have learnt the song from Paul Clayton, but if so it took a form Clayton adopted after recording the song for his 1957 Folkways 10" album, *Cumberland Mountain Folksongs*. Clayton was a friend of Dylan's - they had gigged together as recently as September (perhaps Clayton taught him the song at this point) - and would later become the acknowledged source for the tunes to Dylan's own 'Don't Think Twice, It's All Right' and 'Percy's Song'. He was a keen folklorist, as well as a folksinger whose attitude to his material he defined as, "a professional folksinger working with public audiences ought to present the best text and tune."[3] Sadly, Clayton took his own life in April 1966.

Though Dylan's version is significantly less garbled than most twentieth century renditions, it raises its own set of questions. In Dylan, the identity of the mysterious stranger is stated explicitly at the outset - "a ghost come back from out in the sea" - begging a query: what motive does the ghost have for his 'theft' of the house carpenter's wife? Certainly not the same as a mortal lover returned. And why would Dylan feel the need to explain the stranger's identity in a way all but unknown in American tradition, highlighting the supernatural aspect of the stranger unless, that is, "something has been lost" over centuries of oral transmission?

Perhaps even more perplexing, to me at least, was the dialogue that concludes Dylan's rendition - the visions of the hills of heaven and hell - implying that the "ghost" intends to punish the house-carpenter's wife for some wrong, real or imagined, by making her join him in hell. What would warrant such an eternity of damnation and why did all the other versions I had referenced as possible sources omit such dramatic dialogue? The almost ubiquitous finale to recordings of 'House Carpenter', one happily adopted by the likes of Dyer-Bennett, Ashley and Gladden, was a simple cuss at the folly of womankind and the amorality of your average sea-farer:

> A curse be on the sea-faring men,
> Oh, cursed be their lives,
> For they are robbing the House-Carpenter
> And coaxing away their wives.[4]

Even Paul Clayton's finale, though it contained no such curse and

4

moan, took the form of a bulletin, notifying the house carpenter of impending tragedy:

> Straight news, straight news, to the house carpenter,
> Straight news, straight news, back to land,
> The ship that your wife is sailing on
> Is sinking under the sand.[5]

Just one possible conduit had a version sharing the same denouement as Dylan's, one I found hiding in the deep recesses of a 1988 various artist compilation of Dylan's 'revivalist' contemporaries, *Blues In The Bottle*. Dave Van Ronk in the summer of 1961 - before their falling out, the result of Dylan's appropriation of Van Ronk's arrangement of 'House of the Rising Sun' - was one of Dylan's most willing resources of tradition. His version of 'The House Carpenter' postdates Dylan's, being recorded sometime in 1964, but Van Ronk would have already known the song and could easily have taught it to Dylan first-hand. On the released cut Van Ronk refrains from any spoken intro. and, though he does sing of "banks of sweet Italy" and hills of heaven and hell, his phraseology is slightly different from Dylan's:

> What hills, what hills are those, my dear,
> What hills so fair and high?
> Those are the hills of heaven, my dear,
> But not for you or I.
>
> What hills, what hills are those, my love
> What hills so dark and low?
> Those are the hills of hell, my dear,
> Where you and I must go.[6]

Though the "fair and high"/"dark and low" dichotomy does not tally with Dylan, a common source seemed probable, at least until I questioned Van Ronk. The bearded behemoth informed your intrepid reporter that he had learnt the song in the mid-Fifties from Buell Kazee. Kazee, a minister born in a log house in Magoffin County, Kentucky, learnt many a song from his mother who "sang Elizabethan ballads over the dish water."[7] Between the years 1926 and 1930 Kazee made some fifty-two recordings for Brunswick and Vocalion. However, he would not make any further official recordings until 1958 and none of the known 78s has yet to yield a 'House Carpenter'. Though Van Ronk may well have learnt the song first-hand from Kazee, it is highly unlikely that Dylan would have followed suit, and Van Ronk assured me he did not teach the song to Dylan himself. Dead-end. I turned around and headed back to the starting point.

To find out how Dylan came upon this take on a four hundred-year old British ballad, I found it necessary to examine three quite separate strands of 'The House Carpenter', in print and in tradition, as they travelled across the Atlantic (and down the centuries), preserved by the semi-literate, collected by the literati. Unravelling the ghost's identity and the wrong for which he was seeking retribution not only brought me closer to an original 'Dæmon Lover'. I also felt myself to be at something like the source for "the only true, valid death you can feel today."

So here is a book that started out as a footnote - from whom did Dylan learn 'The House Carpenter'? - became in turn a brief essay about Dylan's instinctual sense for the most appropriate traditional sources and, finally (and a tad reluctantly), evolved into an investigation into the roots from which all Anglo-American traditional song have been cultivated - all from that starting point of one man, one song, one performance.

The various academic debates on ballad origins and the vagaries of the oral process, by which ballads commonly pass down, must inevitably impinge upon my endeavours, though hopefully not in such a way as to hinder the general reader's enjoyment of what I deem to be a kind of literary detective story. Much "metaphysical moonshine" (to cop a phrase from Bertrand Bronson) may need to be consumed before the clarity of dawn comes. As to my *raison d'etre* for such a curious endeavour, I can quote no better authority than the editor of the very first 'traditionalist' text of 'The Dæmon Lover' to be published, Sir Walter Scott:

> **The study ... of lays rescued from the gulf of oblivion must in every case possess considerable interest for the moral philosopher and general historian ... [and] to the lovers and admirers of poetry as an art, it cannot be uninteresting to have a glimpse of the National Muse in her cradle, or to**

hear her babbling the earliest attempts at the formation of the tuneful sounds with which she was afterwards to charm posterity. [8]

- Clinton Heylin. December 31, 1997.

(i) The Pop Junk of Urban Britain.

> The thirty years in which [Bill] Haley's recording, ['Rock Around The Clock',] has remained at some level of cultural significance - even if it has only an antiquarian aura to it today - is hardly a blip on the history of popular song ... [compared with] a song that was *really* popular, one which has lasted some 330 years (sic), crossed the Atlantic and then crossed back again, and is still sung ... That song is 'The Distressed Ship-Carpenter' or 'The House Carpenter'. - Dave Harker[1]

> Street balladry, the roots of traditional American music, was pop. The purest mountain airs, lustily pursued by sweaty, obsessive folklorists and concerned young things, were once the pop junk of urban Britain ... Street balladry didn't really die at the end of the nineteenth century. Its center became America, instead of Great Britain. - Nick Tosches[2]

Pop sociologists would have us believe that popular music was born somewhere between the invention of the phonograph by Thomas Edison in 1877 and the day that Elvis Presley walked into Sun studios in 1954, depending on whether their personal affiliations may be rock, pop, blues or jazz. In fact the earliest lyric in the English language - 'Sumer is icumen in' - dates from the first half of the thirteenth century; while the first ballads to deal with a definite historical event depict the Battle of Otterburn in 1388 (there are three quite distinct ballads, two extant as mid-sixteenth century manuscripts but undoubtedly originating in the previous milieu).

As William Chappell has written of 'Sumer is icumen in', "the sweet and pastoral character of the melody, in perfect accordance with the sentiments of the words, is indicative of a popular origin"[3]; that 'Chevy Chase', the most manufactured of the Otterburn ballads, evinced a similar popularity can be attested by Addison who, as late as 1711, in a famous article in *The Spectator*, attested that "the old song of 'Chevy Chase' is the favourite ballad of the common people of England."[4]

Dave Harker, an English Marxist with a queen bee in his bonnet about the 'fakelore' that is ballad-studies, and Nick Tosches, an American still hunting for the wellsprings of Americana, are two rare contemporary

8

commentators who have sought to give the history of popular music a wide enough latitude, geographically and chronologically. Unfortunately the two examples they select in order to precis their different agendas - 'The Distressed Ship Carpenter' and 'Gypsy Davey' - do not affirm the importance or durability of the street, or broadside, ballad - they deny it. Not only did neither 'The Distressed Ship Carpenter' nor 'Gypsy Davey' begin life as a street-ballad (I subscribe to Tosches' view that the ultimate source for 'Gypsy Davey' may well be a condensed romance, 'King Orfeo'), but the vibrant oral tradition that kept these two songs alive for some four hundred years existed in determined opposition to street-ballads, i.e. ballads sold by hawkers in the streets of England and America until the tip end of the nineteenth century. Contact with print usually signalled the death of a particular strain of these 'popular ballads'.

Both ballads appear to be the product of a peculiarly British sensibility that originated at the onset of the Renaissance but died on the withered stalk of Reason (the Age, that is) - a spontaneous outburst, perhaps the first, of genuinely popular songmaking.

The central focus of my quest is the very ballad Harker singled out, the story of 'The Distressed Ship Carpenter', better known from Walter Scott's published version as 'The Dæmon Lover' but most commonly identified in folk circles as 'The House Carpenter'. My primary concern is not Harker's skewered views of popular balladry - nor, indeed, Tosches' commendable attempt to relate the birth of 'Country' to a parent British tradition. It is to follow a popular ballad back from the point when it impacted on modern 'pop' forms - specifically the Rockpopfolk melange that Bob Dylan spawned - to its 'original' template, if such a template can be discerned (and conventional ballad wisdom says it cannot), hoping that I shall not be as one with the little boy standing at the side of the road at the end of 'The Ballad of Frankie Lee & Judas Priest', muttering "Nothing is revealed."

Whatever that original template may have been (and template is a term I employ to separate the idea of a constructed text of original motifs from that "scholarly mirage ... a perfectly pure traditional text"[5]), none of the main characters in our story seem entirely sure what our tale is meant to reveal. For Dylan, the ballad told "a story about a ghost come back from

9

out in the sea, come to take his bride away from the house carpenter";
for Robert Graves, "the ghost, disguised in flesh and blood ... took her
aboard a phantom ship which sank as soon as it gained the open sea ...
[having] promised to show her 'where the lilies grow at the bottom of the
sea'"[6]; for Professor Child, "a sort of vulgar rationalism ... [has been
used] to explain the eery personality and proceedings"[7]; for Sir Walter
Scott "it contains a legend, which, in various shapes, is current in
Scotland ... in which a fiend is introduced paying his addresses to a
beautiful maiden"[8]; for seventeenth century poetaster Laurence Price it
was simply 'A warning for Married Woman'. Some have stood on the
brink of its true import, few have had it in them to peer over the
precipice.

But then a sense of narrative dislocation is common enough in any
traditional ballad travelling through unsullied oral tradition for 250 years
or more. As it is, our ballad was not collected from a traditional singer
until 1803, by one William Laidlaw, engaged to collect material on
Scott's behalf for his *Minstrelsy Of The Scottish Border*. And yet if 'The
Dæmon Lover' had to be placed in a specific *milieu*, reflecting a
particular world picture, it would be one we may have seen sifted
through Shakespeare's literary siv but in the ballad form affords the
most authentic reflection available of the Elizabethan popular
imagination.

Published in 1812 by Scott, and henceforth a perennial favourite of
literary anthologists, 'The Dæmon Lover' has also been collected some
two hundred and fifty times from oral tradition, each variant representing
a possible conduit back to some original strain of the story or, like as not,
the dead-end of a printed broadside, as which it has enjoyed three quite
distinct incarnations: 'James Harris' in the seventeenth century, 'The
Distressed Ship Carpenter' in the early eighteenth century (both in
England) and, in its most popular guise, as 'The House Carpenter' in
nineteenth century America.

'The House Carpenter' is an example of what Harvard professor,
Francis J. Child, defined as the popular (or primitive) ballad, a member
of Child's select 305-song canon. By the time he rerecorded the song,
in March 1970, Dylan may have even checked his copy of Child's five
volumes of British balladry, *English & Scottish Popular Ballads*,

10

published between 1882 and 1898, a copy of which Allen Ginsberg once confirmed to me took pride of place on the shelves of Dylan's MacDougall Street townhouse. If so, he would have found the song he recorded listed as Child ballad 243 - but under the title 'James Harris (The Dæmon Lover)'. Child, in defining his canon of ancient British ballads, made a hugely difficult task even more problematic by his determination - with the ballads he chose and the textual parallels to international folklore he did document - to place the origins of the popular ballad not merely at the birth of popular culture, but of culture itself:

> The *popular* ballad, for which our language has no unequivocal name, is a distinct and very important species of poetry. Its historical and natural place is anterior to the appearance of the poetry of art, to which it has formed a step, and by which it has been regularly displaced, and, in some cases, all but extinguished ... The primitive ballad ... is popular, not in the sense of something arising from and suited to the lower orders of a people. As yet, no sharp distinction of high and low exists, in respect to knowledge, desires and tastes.[9]

Child's idealistic conception of ballad origins has not survived as untarnished as his canon of ballads. Nobody seriously believes that "there are some narrative poems in Anglo-Saxon which, without stretch of language, might be called ballads," nor that, "such ballads ... are [simply] lost."[10] More simply, they never existed.

But then as Robert Graves reminds us, "distinctions between the song and narrative ballad, and between the oral and the literary ballad ... did not exist until recent times,"[11] indeed until William Shenstone remarked to Bishop Percy in 1761, "It is become habitual to me to call that a Ballad which describes or implies some Action ... I term that a Song, which contains only an Expression of Sentiment."[12]

Perhaps surprisingly, given the lack of historical veracity that now attaches to his notion of ballad origins, Child's demarcation of the 'popular' ballad - as opposed to the imitative broadside and literary forms of balladry - has remained largely intact. Shenstone's simple distinction between ballad and song did not satisfy Child, nor his apostles (of whom Graves was one). Robert Graves in *The English*

11

Ballad provided eight requirements (actually nine, but he later recanted the ninth, 'communal composition') for the truly popular ballad or, to use his phrase, "the ballad proper":

1. The ballad-proper has no known author.
2. There is never an authoritative text of such a ballad.
3. It is incomplete without music, music of a repetitive kind that excites and sustains.
4. Though it may treat of Kings and Queens and notable figures in history, it is local, not cultural.
5. It is oral, not literary.
6. It is not highly advanced technically.
7. It does not moralize or preach or express any partisan bias.
8. It "begins in the last act" of the drama and moves to the final climax without stage directions.[13]

If these are as useful as such generalities can be, point six strikes me as churlish (and not bourne out by the likes of 'Sir Patrick Spens' or 'The Gaberlunyie Man', two ballads Graves included in his 1957 collection, *English & Scottish Ballads*). My immense respect for Graves' learning will also not dissuade me from chipping away at notion one, drilling holes in seven and eight and even applying the odd depth charge to notion two.

To make anonymity a pre-condition of "the ballad-proper" seems absurd. The traditional ballads that have come down to us *are* 'anonymous' but only, as A.L. Lloyd has correctly observed, by "economic accident". If a recently excavated historical document gave us a name for the author of 'Tam Lin' it would not make the ballad any less traditional. Indeed, 'The Gaberlunyie Man', a ballad unquestionably steeped in tradition, has long been attributed by oral tradition to James V of Scotland, and at least five Child ballads do have attributed authors, three to the same seventeenth century poetaster, Laurence Price - a key figure in our story.

To suggest that a ballad like 'The Dæmon Lover' (one of Graves' own selections for his 1957 collection) - which ends with a ghost punishing a former lover for some wrong done to him by taking her down to hell - "does not moralize" seems a tad flawed as premises go (though preach

12

it does not). Graves' "last act of the drama" precept is just as flawed. A classic popular ballad like 'Young Hunting' unfolds like a grand dramatic production:

Act One - Young Hunting informs a former lover that he loves someone "thrice better than thee."
Act Two - The lady in question gets Young Hunting drunk and takes him to bed and, having made love, stabs him to death.
Act Three - As she tries to decide what to do with the body, she finds herself accused of the murder by a "bonny bird", seemingly inhabited by the soul of the dead man. She attempts to cajole the bird to "light down" with promises of a golden cage. Instead he flies away to seek out the king.
Act Four - The lady throws the body into the river/a well as the bird flies into the king's boudoir to tell of the murder of Young Hunting.
Act Five - When the king visits the lady to ask of Young Hunting's whereabouts, she insists that she has not seen him. Candles, though, are used to locate the body in the river, at which point the lady accuses her maid of the murder.
Act Six - The maid is tied to a stake but the fire will not light.
The lady is then tied to the stake in her place and "her fair body ... burnt like hoky-gren."

The corrupt American form, 'Love Henry', recorded by Dylan in 1993 from a text collected in Alabama in the summer of 1945, has become unduly condensed, but even it does not "begin in the last act of the drama." Rather, 'Love Henry' begins in the first act and ends in the third, as the lady seeks to entice the accusing bird down (any suggestion of young Hunting's soul returning in bird form - an act of metampsychosis - having all but disappeared). What the bird shall do with the information is never resolved. Scholars in love with the efficacy of the 'oral process' - i.e. purely oral transmission of works of 'literature' - often beguile themselves into believing such condensations are necessary excisions by 'the popular mind':

This tendency to concentrate on climactic action is a contribution of the folk to ballad style and form, for it develops in a given ballad as that ballad comes down in time from folk singer to folk singer. Ballads are things of growth; in their earliest forms many, but certainly not all, of the

ballads probably told stories as detailed as any conventional narrative; but as they are recreated by the folk, the slow elements and the undramatic elements are dropped and only the hard core of tension remains.[14]

The example of 'Love Henry' is an appropriate one since, like 'The Demon Lover', it appears to have thrived in Scottish tradition for 300 years and then suddenly dropped from its audible voice, only to reappear in America in the twentieth century, excavated as part of a surprisingly large store of transplanted British ballads. However, the curious practise of using "corpse-lights", a belief in metampsychosis and the barbaric trial by fire at song's end were never going to survive the journey into the hills of Virginia.

Unfortunately the oral process has not provided the only potentially deleterious input into original ballad templates. The popular ballad may have largely confined itself to the oral process until the eighteenth century - save for the occasional ballad that passed muster for broadside purposes - but songsters and garlands increasingly claimed the more popular variants and interred them in wooden blocks of print.

From 1765 literary antiquarians - and their successors, the folklorists - also began to collect ballads "from the mouths of the people." Unfortunately, the viscitudes of a couple of hundred years of creative oral tradition were hard to reconcile with the disparate texts such figures collected and so - presupposing a discernible archetype beneath the bastardized forms sung to them - the literati began to 'literatize' the simple, direct phrases of the common folk, causing one later collector to observe:

> **The tear and wear of three centuries will do less mischief to the text of an old ballad among the vulgar, than one short hour will effect, if in the possession of some sprightly and accomplished editor of the present day.[15]**

And yet this methodology was the very basis on which nearly all the early ballad scholars worked, ever since Bishop Percy's *Reliques of Ancient English Poetry* ("the most important book of poetry published in the 18th century" - Robert Graves[16]) brought ballad-studies to the altar of public awareness in 1765. The one contemporary exception was a

14

fastidious antiquarian named Joseph Ritson.

In many ways, the history of 'ballad studies' might be termed a battle between the sons of Percy, the 'popularizers' seeking a large audience for ballads and (their own) ballad collections, and the sons of Percy's ascerbic nemesis, Ritson, who spent most of his adult life railing against Percy's editorial techniques and never stinted in his determination to make Percy pay for his condescending opening remarks in *Reliques*, and a methodology that was their inevitable by-product:

> **In a polished age, like the present, I am sensible that many of these reliques of antiquity will require great many allowances to be made for them ... Select ballads in the old Scottish dialect, most of them of the first-rate merit, are interspersed [herein] among those of our ancient English minstrels; and the artless productions of these old rhapsodists are occasionally confronted with specimens of the composition of contemporary poets of a higher class.**[17]

Ritson, in the introduction to his own *Select Collection Of English Songs*, referred to "the inaccurate and sophisticated manner in which every thing that had real pretensions to antiquity has been printed by the right reverend editor ... [such that] they who look into it to be acquainted with the state of ancient poetry will be miserably disappointed or fatally misled."[18] Ritson had thrown down a gauntlet to future generations. The belated publication of Percy's famous folio in 1868 finally resolved the "truth of this charge" - in Ritson's favour. In no way had Percy published "the[se] artless productions" as he had found them.

Unfortunately for Ritson and his school, the 'popularizers' have consistently provided for the more distinguished company: the likes of Percy himself, Robert Burns, Sir Walter Scott, Sir Arthur Quiller-Couch and, perhaps surprisingly in the light of his ballad 'divisions', Robert Graves. In both his 1927 *The English Ballad* and his 1957 *England & Scottish Ballads*, Graves, when in doubt, tended to prefer the texts of previous 'popularizers'. The crime these 'popularizers' continued to commit in the eyes of the Ritsonites was to search for that 'authoritative' text and, failing in their task, as they were doomed to do, sought to construct one from the (often meagre) resources at hand. Sigurd Hustvedt recognized the idealistic source of their tamperings in his

15

Ballad Books & Ballad Men (1930):

> A simple explanation of why so many of the older collectors of ballads improved what they found and failed to account properly for their own creative participation, might be that they were subtly led into a mistaken idealism: admiring ballads themselves, they created in their own minds a sort of ballad archetype and so were brought under an irresistible temptation to make ballads which they saw to be imperfect comform more nearly to a visionary ideal.[19]

Figures like Bishop Percy and Sir Walter Scott, having collected various versions of popular ballads, could not resist mixing their own quills' ink with the anonymous authors' lifeblood - even though these elements rarely coagulated into something able to "conform ... to a visionary ideal." Of equal misfortune is the fact that amendations were rarely highlighted and, though manuscripts have been released posthumously, the sources for some of the most anthologized popular ballads (Percy's own 'Sir Patrick Spens', 'Edward' and 'Sir Hugh' being perhaps the most notorious) remain unresolved to this day. In the case of 'The Dæmon Lover', though Scott's has remained the most famous text, his source-text - presumed to be from one Walter Grieve - has not come down to us.

Francis J. Child, the most notable of Ritson's acolytes, made it his goal to get behind the published texts and back to the actual versions collected. Under his guiding light the 'popularizers' were banished into the netherlands of the popular anthology. If Child believed in the efficacy of the manuscript, his work - which collected 1,262 (largely tuneless) texts of (to his mind, the) 305 popular British ballads - inspired a slew of ballad-hunters to track down variants directly from oral tradition. Between the publication of Child's final volume, in 1898, and the death of Cecil Sharp in 1924 the 'first folk revival' remained largely the preserve of these ballad-hunters, figures like Alan Lomax, Sharp himself, Sabine Baring-Gould and the Scottish collectors Reverend J.B. Duncan and Gavin Greig, the last of whom summarized the revivalists' *modus operandi* thus:

> Our main purpose is, in a broad sense, scientific. We want to understand folk-song and to read its message. For this end we must, to

begin with, collect as large a body of folk-songs as possible, in order that we may have material for generalisation. Then we must see that we have the undiluted article. We must in collecting take just what we find, and, in our record, give exactly what we get ... This plan of going to oral and traditional sources marks the new folk-song movement. A good deal of the ink used by Ritson, Chappell, Glen, and others, in fighting over the question of the nationality of songs, might have been saved, had they depended less on the testimony of books and manuscripts, and gone more to oral and traditional sources for their information and for the material from which to construct their theories.[20]

In this fever-pitch of folkdom - which in America did not come to an end until the onset of the Second World War - collectors armed with their list of Child ballads searched north, south, east and west, according these items primacy over all homespun and latespun ballads (exceptions like John Lomax managed to hide their populist tendencies beneath an academic gown). Though such a blinkered approach might be lamented at this late date, thousands of texts AND tunes for Child ballads were collected (to the likes of Sharp the tune always remained 'the thing'), giving post-Child academics and collectors an unprecedented treasure trove of information as to the winding ways of tradition. Here was the body of texts necessary "in order that we may have material for generalisation."

And yet few such generalized expositions have drawn on this vast body of texts and tunes. A.L. Lloyd's level-headed *Folk Song In England* (1967) at least provided a plausible context for the 'second' folk revival. Sharp's own exposition, *English Folk Song: Some Conclusions*, dating from the tender years of his collecting (1907), ten years before any of his excavations in the Appalachian mountains, was quickly found to be wanting but never overhauled. Louise Pound's determinedly savage *Poetic Origins & The Ballad* finally nailed down the communalists' coffins. But these were essentially old debates, with old information. As notable a ballad-scholar as the late Betrand Bronson, whose four-volume *Traditional Tunes Of The Child Ballads* (1959-72) remains an essential addendum to Child (it actually dwarfs its more famous ancestor in both scope and size), never composed a cogent critique of balladry beyond the occasional article formed within a series of microcosms (collected in *The Ballad As Song*).

The entry for Child Ballad No. 243 in *English & Scottish Popular Ballads* [ESPB] comprised just eight texts: two English broadsides, and six renditions collected from oral tradition in Scotland in the early nineteenth century. Post-Child, there have been just five texts collected in Britain (two in Scotland, two in England, one in the Isle of Man), four of which qualify as no more than fragments. Even when the song was collected in the early 1800s by Scottish collectors Peter Buchan, William Laidlaw, William Motherwell, Robert Scott and George Kinloch, it was already passing from the mouths of Scottish ballad singers.

Indeed Child has not been alone in believing that popular balladry itself was largely moribund in Britain by the time he began his great work, though the later volumes of ESPB appeared in direct competition with the early collections of English field-collectors Lucy Broadwood, Frank Kidson and Sabine Baring-Gould. Despite one popular biographer's recent claim that "Child was determined to preserve the rich oral tradition of indigenous folk music ... notating the songs wherever and whenever he found them on his travels,"[21] not once in his forty years-plus of study is there any suggestion Child ever encountered a living folk song, sung by a flesh and blood folksinger. In one fleeting moment of doubt, in 1879, he *did* write to his old friend, the writer James Russell Lowell, asking rhetorically:

> **A recent discovery of an Odinic song in Shetland has excited me very much. I have written the person said to be the right man, to ask what hope there is of ballads. It seems to me they must linger there ... I almost said I would come out: but I reflected upon the state of my pocket, and asked - had I not better spend the £50 it would cost me for the sea passages in buying the help of some poor Shetland schoolmasters or parsons? Only if I were on the spot - that is on the 20 or 30 inhabited islands - I could be continually prodding up the people. There *must* be ballads there: how else have the people held out against poverty, cold & darkness?[22]**

But Child never did "come out" of his cloisters. Even a reference to an American version of 'The House Carpenter' cited in an 1858 edition of *Graham's Illustrated Magazine* (two verses from an American broadside published the previous year) failed to convince Child that a thriving tradition was just outside his front door.

By the time the likes of Dylan came along, the second 'folk revival' - inspired, if Robert Cantwell is to be believed, by the Kingston Trio's innocuous rendition of 'Tom Dooley' - was dissolving many an academic debate. By adding originality to the equation, preferring to recreate rather than replicate tradition, Dylan and his kind once again reminded people that the likes of 'The House Carpenter' could be connected to a living tradition (**Bob Dylan:** You know, many people didn't want to hear it if you couldn't play the song exactly the way that Aunt Molly Jackson played it. I just kind of blazed my way through all that stuff.[23]).

'The House Carpenter', long disappeared from British oral tradition, had dug deep into American soil. Collected some two hundred times from backwoods singers in the trawl of tradition undertaken in the wake of Child, and sharing the A-list of collected Child ballads - along with 'Barbara Allen' and 'Lord Thomas and Fair Eleanor' - it was a staple of most singing revivalists, who saw themselves as part of some 'imagined village' stretching back through the proverbial mists of time. A song like 'The House Carpenter' seemed to connect them to its very foundation stones. The question of how such a self-evidently powerful ballad had disappeared entirely from British tradition was a moot one for any revivalist wavering his or her way through some broadside derivative.

Sadly, the song s/he now sang was an estranged grandchild from a once noble family or, in balladic terms, a fuzzy xerox of a 10" x 8" culled from a copy negative. The contradictions have remained unresolved too long, perhaps by those wise enough to see the tangents such a search may require:

> O see ye not yon narrow road,
> So thick beset wi' thorns and briers?
> That is the Path of Righteousness,
> Though after it but few inquires.[24]

(ii) A Very Moderate Jewel.

The immense collections of Broadside ballads, the Roxburghe and Pepys [collections], of which but a small part has been printed, doubtless contains some ballads which we should at once declare to possess the popular character, and yet on the whole they are veritable dung-hills, in which, only after a great deal of sickening grubbing, one finds a very moderate jewel. - Francis J. Child.[1]

The interplay between traditional ballads and broadside ballads through the centuries has long been a fierce forum for debate, scholars often choosing to pour scorn on any ballads that first found solace among the penny-sheets. Child's outburst to the Danish scholar Svend Grundtvig, above, reflects the view of most ballad scholars. Its underlying assumption? That no traditional song which fell into the hands of the blackletter press emerged unscathed. And yet the broadside press can never be entirely disregarded as a source of traditional fare. Child himself, after dismissing the "veritable dung-hills" of English broadsides, found room for 106 such "moderate jewels" - sixty two of which provide the prime or sole version [cf. Roy Palmer's useful article in the 1996 *Folk Music Journal*, "Veritable Dunghills: Professor Child and the Ballad"] - among his 305 popular ballads.

Unfortunately for Child, the broadside 'variants' of the 106 such "moderate jewels" he chose to include in his collection almost invariably prove to be the earliest published texts, in some cases predating the first oral transcription by a couple of centuries. Such is the case with 'The House Carpenter' or 'Dæmon Lover', making the broadsides a necessary starting-point for our investigations - as well as affording one of the best examples of the ways broadsides both preserve and pervert the course of tradition.

The first time a close relative of Dylan's 'House Carpenter' definitely appeared in print was in a substantial anthology of over a thousand songs printed in London circa 1737-38. On page 466 of *A Collection Of Diverting Songs* can be found a ballad bearing the title, 'The Ship Carpenter's Wife' (commonly reprinted as 'The Distressed Ship-Carpenter'). The only surviving copy of the volume in question now resides at the Bodliean Library in Oxford. It runs to some fourteen verses, six of which find parallells in Dylan's rendition.

It is highly unlikely that the song was collected first-hand by the compiler of *A Collection Of Diverting Songs*. On the evidence of the other songs that comprise this tome (at least those I have been able to cross-reference), most if not all of our compiler's texts were taken from published sources. The editor was almost certainly simply responding to the market for such popular collections opened up by the likes of Thomas D'Urfey's six-volume *Pills To Purge Melancholy* [1719-20], Allan Ramsay's three-volume *Tea-Table Miscellany* [1724-27] and the anonymous *A Collection Of Old Ballads* [1723-24]. As such, his sources are likely to have been those that came easiest to hand.

This is what separates our anonymous compiler from eighteenth century antiquarians like Bishop Percy, Samuel Johnson and William Shenstone; that, whereas they generally scorned such sources as broadsides and/or garlands, these items seem to have provided the editor of *A Collection Of Diverting Songs* with just about all the texts he required. He was certainly no Percy, a man who drew the texts for his 1765 collection primarily from manuscripts and correspondence. This raises the possibility, I would say the likelihood, that 'The Ship-Carpenter's Wife' existed as a broadside prior to its 1737 anthologizing (many a late seventeenth century broadside, a fair few cited in the Stationers' Register, have eluded the grasp of the historically-inclined).

Though it remains impossible to establish, save by inference, the oral currency of 'The Distressed Ship Carpenter' "among common people" at this time, if the song did exist as a broadside in the late seventeenth century then it becomes possible to extend its life in English print for a hundred years or more. It certainly enjoyed a series of late eighteenth century reprints in thirteen-verse form as part of *The Rambler's Garland*. Though the earliest publishing date for the *Rambler's Garland* text is around 1785, it was from this source that Child derived his B text for the ballad. It may well have been Child's lack of awareness of a published version some fifty years earlier that originally led him to query the song's traditional provenance (of which more later).

21

The broadside form remained as popular in America as in England throughout the eighteenth and nineteenth centuries, and examples abound of British broadsides reprinted *verbatim* by American presses. However, any American reprint of 'The Ship Carpenter's Wife' remains undocumented. As such, even though the ballad may have been carried overseas in broadside or chapbook form, in the years between its arrival in the States and a mid-nineteenth century American broadside it must have survived in oral tradition, where each variant would have been required to compete with others over yon hill. Whether that period in an American oral tradition unaffected by the printed word extended a couple of decades or a couple of centuries we know not, but either its first appearance in American print coincided with a remarkable renaissance among traditional singers in the New World, or it was by 1850 already a revered specimen of Old World values.

The so-called De Marsan broadside, actually first published by De Marsan's predecessor J. Andrews in New York circa 1857 - and rapidly adopted by American printers of songsters and broadsides like Delaney and Wehamn - seems to have played a large part in any mini-revival, at the same time loosening the grip of all previous templates on American tradition. Of the 200+ versions collected in America in the twentieth century, not even a handful omit this text's unmistakeable watermark.

In other words, this nineteenth century American broadside, a descendant of a late seventeenth-century English broadside, has been almost entirely responsible for the song's survival, and the form of its survival, in twentieth century tradition. However, a comparison of the two broadside texts also illustrate certain trademarks of oral tradition in the hundred and twenty years that separate the two printings. In De Marsan's text, the turns of phrase have been modernized and colloquialized by a number of hands, not one. At the same time it has become entangled with a separate strain of our ballad, of provenance unknown, represented by three 'new' verses [3, 6 and 10]:

1. Well met, well met, my own true love Long time have I been seeking thee, I'm lately come from the Salt Seas And all for the sake, love, of thee	1. Well met, well met, my own true love Well met, well met, cried he, For I've just returned from the salt sea And all for the love of thee.

22

DYLAN'S DAEMON LOVER

2.I might have had a King's daughter,
And fain would she have married me,
But [I] forsook those crowns of gold
And it's all for the sake, love, of thee.

3. If you might have had a King's daughter,
I think [that] you [are] much to blame,
I would not for five hundred pounds
That my husband should know of the same.

4. For my husband is a Carpenter
And a young ship-carpenter is he,
And by him I have a little son,
Or else, love, I'd go along with thee.

5.But if I should leave my husband dear.
And my little son also,
What have you to maintain me withal,
If I along with you should go?

6.I have seven ships upon the seas
And one of them brought me to land,
And [17] mariners to wait on thee
And to be, love, at your command.

7. A pair of slippers thou shalt have
They shall be made of beaten gold,
Nay and be lin'd with velvet so soft,
For to keep thy soft feet from the cold.

2. I might have married a king's daughter,
....

....
You might have married her, cried she,
 For I am married to a house-carpenter,
And a fine young man is he!

3. If you will forsake your House-Carpenter,
And go along with me,
I will take you to where the grass grows high
On the banks of old Tennessee!

4.If I forsake my House-Carpenter,
And go along with thee,
What have you got to keep me upon,
And keep me from misery?

5.Says he, I've got six ships at sea,
All sailing to dry land,
One hundred & ten of your own countrymen
Love, they shall be at your command.

8. A gilded boat my Love shall have,
With oars like a gilded bow,
And mariners to row thee along,
To keep thee from [thy] overthrow.

6. She took her babe upon her knee
And kissed it one, two and three,
Saying, Stay at home, my darling sweet babe
And keep your father's company!

9. They had not been long upon the seas
Before that she began to weep,
The tears flow'd down her rosy cheeks,
As she walk'd to ond fro the Ship.

7. They had not sailed four weeks or more
Four weeks, or scarcely three,
When she thought of her darling sweet babe at home,
And she wept most bitterly.

10. What, weep you for my Gold? he said
Or do you weep for my fee
Or weep you for some other young man
That loves you better than me?

8. Says he, "Are you weeping for gold, my love,
Or are you weeping for fear,
Or are you weeping for your House-Carpenter
That you left and followed me?

11. I weep not for your gold, she said,
Neither do I weep for my fee
But I do weep for my little son
That should have come along with me.

9. I am not weeping for gold she replied,
Nor am I weeping for fear,
But I am weeping alone for my sweet little babe,
That I left with my house-carpenter.

10. Oh, dry up your tears, my own true love,
And cease your weeping, cried he,
For soon you'll see your own happy home,
On the banks of old Tennessee!

12. She had not been upon the Seas
Passing Days three or four
But the Mariners & she were drowned,
And never were heard of more.

11.They had not sailed five weeks or more,
Five weeks or scarcely four,
When the ship struck a rock and sprang a leak,
And they were never seen any more.

13. When tidings to old England came,
The ship Carpenter's Wife was drown'd;
He wrung his hands and tore his hair:
And most grievously did mourn.

14. Oh cursed be those Mariners!
For they do lead a wretched life,
They ruined [me,] a young Ship-Carpenter
By deluding away his wife.[2]

12. A curse be on the sea-faring men,
Oh cursed be their lives,
For while they are robbing the House-Carpenter;
And coaxing away their wives.[3]

In neither imprint are there any hills of heaven and hell, no supernatural identity to the returned lover, no suggestion that the wife's demise has been orchestrated. Even the 'new' verses provide only a marginally different slant.

That both the returned lover and the wife refer to "my fee" in *A Collection Of Diverting Songs* strongly suggests a mistranscription. Clearly, the "fee" should represent a contrast to the "gold", being her property, not his - this suggests collection from oral tradition. This is significant as the *Diverting Songs* text from 1737 has four lines [highlighted in bold] not represented in more popular, late eighteenth-century reprints, including two which not only complete the dialogue between former lover and ship-carpenter's wife, but represent part of the most durable element of the song in tradition:

> I weep not for your gold, she said,
> Neither do I weep for my fee.

Given the survival of this dialogue complete in the American broadside, the song presumably passed to America from oral tradition or seventeenth-century broadside (*Diverting Songs* having almost no currency itself). The De Marsan broadside mistranscribes the phrase, "weeping for your fee", making it "weeping for fear" - "fear" replacing "fee", an archaic expression usually referring to an inheritance but here presumably referential to the lady's dowry. This suggests a period of transmission in an enviroment where the meaning of the term had been lost.

25

By omitting verses three, four, seven, eight and thirteen from the English broadside, the beguiling of the lady has been reduced to a simple bribe ("One hundred and ten ... shall be at your command") and the ship carpenter denied a voice. Not only has any possible motive for retribution by a supernatural visitation been Typexed (sic) out, but little of substance has taken its place.

And, as it turns out, none of the three verses now introduced into the story are American in origin. Verses three ("If you will forsake your House-Carpenter"), six ("She took her babe upon her knee") and ten ("Oh, dry up your tears, my own true love") all appear in recognizable form in the seven traditional texts collected in Scotland in the early nineteenth century (cf. Child's collection). Verse six parallels one in Walter Scott's text [verse eight]. Verses three and ten, which revolve around the former lover's promise to show the ship carpenter's wife "where the grass grows high/ On the banks of old Tennessee," transliterate a British original, but in such a way as to dissipate the menace implicit in the original 'offer'.

All of the known texts collected from nineteenth century Scottish oral tradition identify the location of the first offer as "the banks of Italy." In Peter Buchan's 1828 text, though, we find two quite contrasting offers. A dislocated sixteenth stanza provides the appropriate parallel for verse three in De Marsan:

BUCHAN	DE MARSAN

O hold your tongue, my sprightly
    flower
Let a' your mourning be;
I'll show you how the lilies
    grow
On the banks o Italy.[4]
	If you will forsake your House-
	    Carpenter,
	And go along with me,
	 I will take you to where the grass
	    grows high,
	On the banks of old Tennessee.

but, unlike verse ten of De Marsan, which simply reiterates the promise, Buchan's resolves itself as:

> I said ye shoud see the lilies grow
> On the banks of Italy;

26

> But I'll let you see the fishes swim,
> In the bottom o the sea.[5]

In Kinloch's ms., contemporary with Buchan (c.1820s), but primarily culled from the Scottish borders rather than the wilder climes of Aberdeenshire, the lover also first profers:

> I'll show whare the white lillies grow,
> On the banks of Italie.[6]

But, as the judgemental nature of the apparition is finally revealed, his offer changes to:

> I'll show where the white lillies grow,
> In the bottom of the sea.[7]

The eminent Mr. Graves, determinedly locating the genesis of popular balladry in a time still essentially pagan, was of the opinion that, "he promised to show her 'where the lilies grow at the bottom of the sea' - not on 'the banks of Italy'" - because "the old pre-Christian Hell was cold, and lay to the far North."[8] In fact, such a notion also appears in Judeo-Christian tradition. In the Book of Isaiah (14:13) Lucifer announces, "I will sit also upon the mount of the congregation, in the sides of the north."

Fleming Andersen, in his *Commonplace & Creativity*(1985), called this technique - that is, "two stanzas framing a scene ... [and] although separated, the two occurences are dependent on each other"[9] - 'narrative repetition'. He also noted that, "Ballad formulas do not often participate in structures of this kind." What it suggests is a degree of literary sophistication on the part of the original composer rare in popular balladry.

The De Marsan broadside drains all the power from these contrasting images. References to "the banks of Italy," when they survive in versions collected from American tradition, invariably indicate a remnant of British oral tradition struggling to cut through some overhauled De Marsan derivative. Unfortunately, evidence of such residual British tradition comes all too rarely from the backwoods of America. Bertrand

27

Bronson's epic anthology of 'text and tunes' to Child ballads, *The Traditional Tunes Of The Child Ballads*, includes 140 versions of 'The House Carpenter' collected from American tradition but just eight such examples that preserve "the banks of Italy." Some other versions offer to show her the banks of the deep, blue sea but it is difficult to know whether this is the result of solid tradition or simply a convenient rhyme. American singers unhappy with the banks of Tennessee have resorted to everything from the "banks of Sweet Willie" to those "of sweet liberty". In Dylan's case, he correctly recalled the "shores of Italy" but, sadly, not its sibling verse, leaving its original import still-born.

The reference to "the banks of Tennessee" clearly implies that the De Marsan broadside derived, at least in part, from oral tradition. The Dylan version appears, at first listen, to consist largely of a condensed De Marsan, but with an ending tagged on from what we'll dub, for now, The Scott Strain. On closer examination, though, its preservation of "the banks of Italy" and, indeed, a correctly restored "fee" suggests an original stream of American tradition from which De Marsan itself had been diverted. Presuming it was the De Marsan virus that muscled in on a Scott-like text, the denouement must have survived simply because it could not be reconciled with De Marsan's ending (which presumably did not as yet have the power of the printed word at its command). The dramatic import of the 'heaven and hell' dialogue certainly provides a stark contrast to the anticlimactic promise to "see your own happy home on the banks of old Tennessee."

That the De Marsan strain of 'House Carpenter' seems to have overwritten many a text that previously drew solace from British oral tradition is truly a damning indictment of what might be termed The Broadside Effect upon traditional processes. Even when there remains evidence of a British oral source underlying an American rendition, the De Marsan gloss has almost always been applied. This makes particularly problematic establishing the form and relative dispersal of texts prevalent in the US at the time of the De Marsan printing. Only by disentangling the broadside elements from 'purer' elements - i.e. those elements preserved in early British oral tradition but unrepresented by any Broadside Imprint - can we continue burrowing towards the original template for Dylan's ghost-ridden 'House Carpenter'. This requires us to recognize that:

28

the conditions under which folk-song had to survive ... [in the U.S. were] unlike those under which it had previously developed ... Instead of being cultivated by a static, homogeneous population, it had to live among people flung together in quite new groups, who had been uprooted from their old enviroments.[10]

That the full *Diverting Songs* text managed to reach America's shores intact is affirmed by a single American source. Bounding forward and westward, we come upon a version collected by Alan and Elizabeth Lomax from Clay Walters in Salyersville, Kentucky, in 1937, which concludes with the English two-verse coda, the only such instance in latterday oral tradition:

> 14. Straight news, straight news to the ship carpenter,
> Straight news come back to the land,
> The ship that his own dear wife sailed in,
> Went sinking to the sand.

> 15. Sailors may be the worst of men,
> That lead poor women astray,
> The sailor has ruined the ship carpenter,
> By deluding his poor wife away.[11]

The first of these verses finds its parallel in Paul Clayton's recording, learnt from the old Virginian Finlay Adams, but the final verse seems to have been unknown to Adams. Walters' use of 'ship carpenter' rather than 'house carpenter' is also all but unknown in American tradition (though it features in the solitary Canadian text collected). Walters also sings two earlier verses parallelled in *Diverting Songs*, yet absent from De Marsan:

WALTERS	DIVERTING SONGS
3. If you could have the king's daughter, dear	If you might have had a king's daughter,
I'm sure that you are to blame	I think that you are much to blame,
For I wouldn't have my husband to hear tell of thee	I would not for 500 pounds
For ten thousand pounds of gold.	That my husband should know of the same.

4. Oh, I am married to a ship carpenter
And a ship carpenter I obey
And by him I have a little son
Or I would go along with thee. [12]

For my husband is a Carpenter
And a young ship-carpenter is he,
And by him I have a little son,
Or else, love, I'd go along with thee.

However, the most intriguing possibility raised by Walters' rendition (which the Lomaxes had the foresight to record - see discography) is that the English broadside itself may have shed some verses along the way. Preceding the moralizing coda are those hills of heaven and hell:

> 12. What hills, what hills, my own true love,
> That look so white like snow?
> It's the hills of Heaven, my own true love
> Where all righteous people go.
>
> 13. What hills, what hills, my own true love,
> That look so dark and low?
> It's the hills of Hell, my own true love,
> Where you and I must go. [13]

Perhaps Walters' printed predecessor was in fact a rationalized substitute for a more surreal original. The Walters rendition certainly seems to be an almost unique example of a 'complete' American text referential to unadulterated British tradition - hence the absence of telltale transitions from ship-carpenter and banks of Italy to house-carpenter and banks of Tennessee. As it is, the moralizing coda that concludes the English broadside, and Clay Walters' text has probably been made to conform to broadside convention by universalizing a very personal curse - that of the ship carpenter. In Peter Buchan's version, collected directly from oral tradition in the nether regions of North-East Scotland in the early 1820s, the song concludes (actually should conclude, as these verses are succeeded by two stock verses of 'divers doggerel', describing the wife's beauty) with:

> The fatal flight o' this wretched maid
> Did reach her own countrie;
> Her husband then distracted ran,

And this lament made he:

"O wae be to the ship, the ship,
And wae be to the sea,
And wae be to the mariners
Took Jeanie Douglas frae me!"[14]

This thrice-woeful cry of the carpenter at song's end has proved to be his only entrance into the ballad to which his name has become inextricably bound. The familiar curse tossed out at the end of the 1857 broadside puts the ship carpenter's curse into a far less satisfactory, third-person form.

Though Clay Walters' rendition also includes two of the three verses in De Marsan not in *Diverting Songs*, it omits any reference to the "banks of Italy." A complete text containing all three 'orally-acquired' verses - drawn from a stream independent of *either* broadside - *has* been collected in twentieth century America. It suggests that a collision between (a derivative of) the English broadside and an entirely separate British oral tradition - resulting in the De Marsan derivative - occured in America before any naturalizing process had taken hold. This rare example of a British undercoat intact can be found in Winston Wilkinson's manuscript, housed at the University of Virginia. Collected by Mr. Wilkinson himself from a Miss Tyrah Lam in Elkton, Virginia in 1935, eight of the first eleven verses accord with the first eight verses of De Marsan. However, verse five preserves our banks of Italy:

If you will leave your house carpenter,
And go along with me.
I'll take you where the grass grows green,
On the banks of sweet Italy.[15]

The denouement, though, entirely omits the moralizing coda, concluding with the increasingly familiar visions of heaven and hell:

12. What hills, what hills, my false true love,
What hills so black and blue?
The hills you see are the hills of Hell,
Awaiting both me and you.

31

13. What hills, what hills, my false true love,
What hills so white as snow?
The hills you see are the hills of Heaven,
Where you and I can't go.[16]

The reader may have started to think that there is nothing unusual about the hills' appearance in American tradition. Not so, my friend. Of the 86 versions in Bronson that qualify as more than fragments, just 14 feature these verses, barely more than those featuring "the banks of Italy."

The Lam text is central to any understanding of the relationship between the American 'House Carpenter' and its British parent. Though verses five and eight correspond to two of the three De Marsan verses unreplicated by the earlier English broadside, the reference to "the banks of sweet Italy" confirms a source preceding the De Marsan transliteration. The surely symbolic couplet, "She turned herself three times around/ And looked at her babies three," otherwise unreplicated in American tradition, suggests perhaps an Old World superstition designed to ward off evil. The reference in the third verse to having "forsaken those crowns of gold," may occur in *A Collection Of Diverting Songs* but it also crops up in Scottish oral tradition - in Motherwell (Child E), as "I refused the crown of gold," and in Buchan (Child C), as "I despised the crown o' gold," while the uniquely English description of golden slippers and gilded boats remains absent.

What we have in Lam are three verses that cannot be traced to either broadside - yet also occur in Walters' *and* Dylan's renditions - integrated into a version containing nine of the De Marsan verses. The similarities between Lam's and Dylan's renditions are striking (all of Dylan's ten verses have their equivalent here, save for his attack of amnesia at the end of verse six), though Lam has lost the anachronistic "fee" and Dylan has not. But it is unlikely Dylan had recourse to a direct derivative of Lam. In Lam's rendition the otherworldy status of the "false true love" (an oxymoron in the true sense) remains implicit at song's end, nor does Dylan provide an equivalent to Lam's second verse, which yields another core constituent of the ballad's most ancient tradition:

O hold your tongue of your former vows,

For they'll bring bitter strifes.
O hold your tongue of your former vows,
For I have become a wife.[17]

This begs an obvious question: what former vows?

(iii) "All For The Sake of Thee"

> You maidens that desire to love
> And would good husbands choose,
> To him that you, by vow, to love
> By no means do refuse,
> For God that hears all secret oaths
> Will dreadful vengeance take,
> On such that of a wilful vow
> Do slender reckoning make. - 17th century broadside.[1]

The importance of the "former vows" to the original tale of 'The Dæmon Lover' cannot be underestimated. In the Virginia text the significance of the vows may have been worn away by tradition - lines one and three presumably originally read, "O hold your tongue of *our* former vows," - but, if so, the change occured before Walter Scott anthologized the song. Save for a second line that reads "for they will breed sad strife," his second verse accords with Lam's in all particulars.

Though these "former vows" are rarely encountered in American tradition, another Stateside text, collected in Eastern Tennessee by Charles Morrow Wilson, reveals the subtext of these vows that irked the dæmon lover so:

> Well met, well met, my own true love,
> Well met, well met, said he.
> Now that the span of years is done
> I'm returnin' to marry thee.
>
> Have you wedded any other man?
> I'm shore I've wed no other woman.
> Yes, I'm wedded to a house carpenter,
> And I think he's a very nice man.
>
> You better leave your house carpenter
> And come along with me;
> We'll go till we come to the old salt sea,
> And married we will be.[2]

So these vows were almost certainly secret vows of marriage, exchanged by two lovers before the male partner took to sea. The binding nature of these vows was highlighted recently by David Atkinson in an article in the *Folk Music Journal*, 'Marriage and Retribution in 'James Harris":

> In early seventeenth-century England, according to ecclesiastical law which regulated such matters, all that was strictly required for the formation of a valid marriage contract was the mutual consent of the two persons involved. The unqualified exchange of consent in words of the present tense, known as spousals *de praesenti*, constituted a marriage contract which was deemed irregular until publicly celebrated in church, but which nonetheless made the couple husband and wife with immediate effect. Any subsequent marriage with another partner would constitute a breach of precontract and be invalid ... Promises of marriage [were] considered in the same light as other vows or oaths sealed by the invocation of God's name, so that to break them involved an act of perjury ...The revenant spirit in [this ballad] ...can be explained as the agent of Providence enacting a divine punishment for the woman's perjury.[3]

Just one other American version preserves these "former vows." Unlike Wilkinson's and Wilson's collected texts, the rendition in question, uncovered in Springfield, Vermont, not only survived uncontaminated by De Marsan and his various proxys but by *any* derivative from *Diverting Songs*. The female repository, one Ellen M. Sullivan, first recollected the song to collector Helen Hartness Flanders on July 13, 1932. All that she remembered was that a, "girl promises to marry a man who goes away, dies and as a ghost returns and says,"

> Oh come with me to the banks of Claudy,
> And perform those promises to me, me.

later in the song:

> When she came to the banks of Claudy,
> Oh, sorry sore was she.
> There were seven ships sailing to the brim.
> They sunk to the bottom and was never seen no more.

> When she came to the banks of Claudy,
> Oh, sorry sore was she, she,
> For the ships they were made of the yellow beaten gold
> And the sails were of silk so fine.[4]

A month later Flanders returned and managed to glean some additional verses. Mrs. Sullivan called the song 'George Allis', and recalled that the girl in the song, "lay asleep and his ghost came to her." She then recalled much the same verse as Miss Lam:

> Oh, begone, begone, young George Allis,
> For I am a married wife,
> Oh, begone, young George, she said,
> For fear there may be strife.

as well as a verse not replicated in any other traditional text, though the second couplet approximates to Morrow Wilson's third verse:

> That is not the promise you gave to me
> To come in seven long years and a day,
> So now come on to the salty seas
> And perform your promises to me.[5]

At last we encounter the evidence that Dylan's "ghost come back from out in the sea" once existed in American tradition. Indeed, in Sullivan's text the ghost came to her in her sleep, placing it in the long-established tradition of revenant ("one who returns after a long absence, esp. the dead"[6]) ballads. The hugely popular "Well met, well met" opening, though, does not fit easily with such a night visitation.

As an intriguing addendum, the version that Mrs. Sullivan sang to Flanders carried a burden, the final line of each verse repeating the final word and then the entire line, thus:

> For fear there may be strife, strife,
> For fear there may be strife.[7]

This rare verse-ending also appears in the version collected by

36

Wilkinson from Miss Lam, this time as a three-word repeat, thus:

> And I think he's a nice young man, man, man,
> And I think he's a nice young man.[8]

perhaps suggesting a connection somewhere down the stream of tradition. Mrs. Sullivan also commented to Flanders that, "He was dead and came back as a ghost after seven years because of the oath that was between them,"[9] making explicit the revenant nature of the dæmon lover and recognizing the 'broken vows' as the song's key motif. This sort of explication is not repeated in American tradition until Mr. Dylan's highly unusual rendition, which also 'reveals' the revenant nature of the 'man' at the outset (though not the "former vows").

Comparison with *A Collection Of Diverting Songs* makes it plain that the 'blame' for a form of rationalization that turned the former lover from revenant to flesh and blood should not be placed at any Yankee's door. It had already occured within the (perhaps exclusively) English strain from which the American broadside largely came. In this rationalized 'English' derivative, the lady does not leave her husband and children without some considerable persuasion on her lover's part; and does so only because of the obligation (and, perhaps, love) she still felt for her former dear. As we shall see, in Scottish oral tradition (and the two American texts that best reflect that tradition) the lady is taken to her death not because she elected to take her lover's proferred escape route - "dying from guilt far from her children,"[10] as Alan Lomax chose to put it - but because she had proved untrue to her former love, having broken the solemn vows she swore some (seven) years before.

The broken vows may be implicit in some twentieth century texts - "I have returned from the salt, salt sea/ And all for the sake of thee" does imply at least some debt of honour ("the love of thee" makes for an inferior reading) - but more traditional texts, of which the renditions collected by Wilkinson, Wilson and Flanders are rare vestiges, make the vow not only explicit, but the veritable crux of our tale.

Perhaps the most extraordinary aspect of the Sullivan text, though, is that she has a name for the revenant, George Allis, seemingly a simple phonetic corruption of the only name ever assigned to the mysterious ex-lover, James Harris (or as Peter Buchan would have it, James Herries). Though it was under this title that the song came to be assigned in Child's *English & Scottish Popular Ballads*, only Buchan called the song by this name.

However, there is a seventeenth-century English broadside commonly known as 'James Harris', though its full title was actually 'A Warning for Married Women, being an example of Mrs Jane Reynolds, a West-country woman, born near Plymouth, who, having plighted her troth to a Seaman, was afterwards married to a Carpenter, and at last carried away by a Spirit, the manner how shall presently be recited' (Snappy, huh!). The broadside in question was first entered in the Stationers Register on 21 February 1657 by Francis Grove (the text in Child dates from a 1685 reprint). This lengthy ditty has none of the compressed drama of 'The Distressed Ship-Carpenter', but it does contain some ancillary details, evidently derived from the 'original' story. As related over its thirty-two stanzas, a familiar tale unfolds, which Child precised thus:

Jane Reynolds and James Harris, a seaman, had exchanged vows of marriage. The young man was pressed as a sailor, and after three years was reported as dead; the young woman married a ship-carpenter, and they lived happily together for four years, and had children. One night when the carpenter was absent from home, a spirit rapped at the window and announced himself as James Harris, come after an absence of seven years to claim the woman for his wife. She explained the state of things, but upon obtaining assurance that her long-lost lover had the means to support her - seven ships upon the sea - consented to go with him, for he was really *much* like unto a man. 'The woman-kind' was seen no more after that; the carpenter hanged himself.[11]

'James Harris' provides a most apposite example of the kind of bowdlerizing perpetrated by blackletter hacks on popular traditional material during the seventeenth and eighteenth centuries. Not surprisingly, 'James Harris' - which in publishing terms represents the starting point for any investigation of 'The Dæmon Lover' - did not pass into any kind of popular (i.e. oral) tradition, British or American, though it stayed a broadside into the eighteenth century (it was last reprinted between 1710 and 1720). One suspects that this failure may, at least partially, have come about because the traditional ballad on which 'James Harris' was based remained in English popular tradition throughout this period. The reader should recognize traces of that antecedent tradition, albeit reflected by texts collected nearly three hundred years later, in the following:

1. There dwelt a fair maid in the West,
Of worthy birth and fame,
Neer unto Plymouth, stately town,
Jane Reynolds was her name.

2. This damsel dearly was belovd
By many a proper youth,
And what of her is to be said
Is known for very truth.

3. Among the rest a seaman brave
Unto her a wooing came;
A comely proper youth he was,
James Harris calld by name.

4. The maid and young man was agreed,
As time did them allow,
And to each other secretly
They made a solemn vow,

5. That they would ever faithfull be
Whilst Heaven afforded life;
He was to be her husband kind,
And she his faithful wife.

6. A day appointed was also
When they was to be married;
But before these things were brought to pass
Matters were strangely carried.

7. All you that faithful lovers be
Give ear and hearken well,
And what of them became at last

I will directly tell.

8. The young man was prest to sea,
And forced was to go;
His sweet-heart she must stay behind,
Whether she would or no.

9. And after he was from her gone
She three years for him stayed,
Expecting of his coming home,
And kept herself a maid.

10. At last news came that he was dead
Within a foreign land,
And how that he was buried
She well did understand,

11. For whose sweet sake the maiden she
Lamented many a day,
And never was she known at all
The wanton for to play.

12. A carpenter that livd hard by,
When he heard of the same,
Like as the other had done before,
To her a wooing came.

13. But when that he had gained her love
They married were with speed,
And four years space, being man and wife,
They lovingly agreed.

14. Three pretty children at this time

This loving couple had,
Which made their father's heart rejoice,
And mother wondrous glad.

15. But as occasion servd, one time
The good man took his way
Some three days journey from his home,
Intending not to stay.

16. But, whilst that he was gone away,
A spirit in the night
Came to the window of his wife,
And did her sorely fright.

17. Which spirit spake like to a man,
And unto her did say,
"My dear and only love," quoth he,
"Prepare and come away.

18. James Harris is my name," quoth he,
"Whom thou didst love so dear,
And I have traveld for thy sake
At least this seven year.

19. And now I am returned again,
To take thee to my wife,
And thou with me shalt go to sea,
To end all further strife."

20. "O tempt me not, sweet James," quoth she,
"With thee away to go;
If I should leave my children small,
Alas! What would they do?

21. My husband is a carpenter,
A carpenter of great fame;
I would not for five hundred pounds
That he should know the same."

22. "I might have had a king's daughter,
And she would have married me;
But I forsook her golden crown,
And for the love of thee.

23. Therefore, if thou'lt thy husband forsake
And thy children three also,
I will forgive thee what is past,
If thou wilt with me go."

24. "If I forsake my husband and
My little children three also,
What means hast thou to bring me to,
If I should go with thee?"

25. "I have seven ships upon the sea;
When they are come to land,
Both mariners and merchandize
Shall be at thy command.

26. The ship wherein my love shall sail
Is glorious to behold;
The sails shall be of finest silk,
And the mast of shining gold."

27. When he had told her these fair tales,
To love him she began,
Because he was in human shape,
Much like unto a man.

28. And so together away they went
From off the English shore,
And since that time the woman-kind
Was never seen no more.

29. But when her husband he come home
And found his wife was gone,
And left her three sweet pretty babes

Within the house alone,

30. He beat his breast, he tore his hair,
The tears fell from his eyes,
And in the open streets he run
With heavy doleful cries.

31. And in this sad, distracted case
He hanged himself for woe
Upon a tree near to the place;
The truth of all is so.

32. The children now are fatherless,
And left without a guide,
But yet no doubt the heavenly powers
Will for them well provide.[12]

That 'James Harris' enjoyed some popularity during the second half of
the seventeenth century is reflected in the number of reprintings.
According to Harker, it was printed up at least seven times between
1657 and 1720, by the likes of F. Coles (1658-64), Gilbertson
(1654-1663), Vere (1640-1680), W. Thackeray & T. Passinger
(1686-1688) and W. Oney (1650-1702)[13]. However, it is hard not to
agree with Sabine Baring-Gould, who, in *Songs From The West*, called it
"a sorry composition" and further noted:

> **The traditional ballad, as compared with the printed ballad, is
> superior at every point [though] it begins abruptly with the address of the
> sailor to the carpenter's wife.[14]**

More contentiously, Baring-Gould held the view that, "the printed ballad
that is in the Roxburgh Collection is ... a clumsy rewriting of the earlier
ballad, so as to convey a moral, as its title implies, 'A Warning to Married
Women'." Though his view was one shared by Robert Graves, who
called 'James Harris', "a late and prosaic English broadsheet [that]
preserves what appears to be the original story,"[15] the Gospel According
to Child designates 'James Harris' as the 'A' text for Ballad #243 (in
organizing his many variants, Child sought to suggest that the A text was

41

not only his preferred text, but also the 'most authentic'). Child says of the traditional Scottish versions:

> **[They] have for their basis the broadside A ['James Harris']; the substance of the story is repeated, with traditional modifications. Two or three stanzas of A are of the popular description, but it does not seem necessary to posit a tradition behind A.**[16]

I beg to differ. It strikes me as not only "necessary to posit a tradition behind A," but quite impossible to arrive at a plausible explanation of the vagaries of subsequent oral tradition without a 'popular' antecedent for the 'James Harris' broadside. Frankly, it was probably Child's lack of first-hand contact with 'the folk process' that led him astray. Positing 'James Harris' as the basis for the traditional ballad of 'The Dæmon Lover', as collected in Scotland, suggests someone well removed from the practicalities of oral disemination. For a broadside ballad like 'James Harris' to have not left a single actual derivative in tradition and still spawned one of the most vibrant popular ballads of all time would certainly require a savage rewrite of any treatises on the oral process currently formulated. And yet few in Child's revered wake have endorsed Baring-Gould's assignment of 'James Harris' as "a clumsy rewriting of [an] earlier ballad."

As it is, Child might well have revised his opinion if he had been made aware that his B text ('The Distressed Ship-Carpenter') was actually first put into published form at least fifty years before his assigned date i.e. 1737, rather than 1785. Even if we permit the editor of *Diverting Songs* credit for its first imprint, we would still be required to believe that between 1657 and 1737 'James Harris' passed into tradition with a particular tune, re-emerging eighty years later, again from tradition, with a new tune, the same tale, but just five of the original thirty-two verses 'intact'. Now integrated into a thirteen-verse ballad, in popular mode, it then passed so rapidly to various climes of Scotland, the west of England, the Isle of Man and America that it could be collected in Scotland sixty-six years later, in supernatural form, and in America - fifty years further on - rerationalized on its return to print, but with elements of the Scottish strain present. Truly an example of "the wonder-working power of tradition!"[17]

The more plausible explanation is that the "two or three stanzas of A [that] are of the popular description" are *taken directly from popular tradition* by the hack responsible for 'James Harris'. Comparing verses in the song "of the popular description" with a handful of those self-evidently not suggests two quite distinct sensibilities: one uncouth and clumsy, the other direct and natural; one overly prosaic, the other unselfconsciously poetic:

This damsel dearly was belovd
By many a proper youth,
And what of her is to be said
Is known for very truth.

A carpenter that livd hard by,
When he heard of the same,
Like as the other had done before
To her a-wooing came.

But when that he had gained her love
They married were with speed,
And four years space, being man and wife,
They lovingly agreed.

I might have had a king's daughter,
And she would have married me;
But I forsook her golden crown,
And [all] for the love of thee.

I have seven ships upon the sea;
When they are come to land,
Both mariners and merchandize
Shall be at thy command.

The ship wherein my love shall sail
Is glorious to behold;
The sails shall be of finest silk
And the mast of shining gold.[18]

Only verses 21,22 and 24-26 of 'James Harris' can be said to have been located in tradition, though the other verses comprising dialogue between the former lovers - i.e. the second half of verse 17, verses 18-20 and 23 - approximate to verses with traditional pedigree. Indeed, by taking verses 17-26 one would have all "the substance of the story" of 'James Harris'. Verses 1-16 and 27-32 seem to exemplify the kind of blackletter embroidery to which the popular (in Child's sense of the word) might be knitted to impress the uncultivated. The author of 'James Harris' surely knew a traditional version of 'The Dæmon Lover' which accorded, in whole or in part, with verses 17-26 and that may, or may not, have had an ending more surreal than the strangely muted:

And so together away they went
From off the English shore,
And since that time the woman-kind
Was never seen no more. [Yeuch!][19]

43

As Baring-Gould observed, this author seems to have had a specific didactic purpose in mind in moulding the traditional tale of 'James Harris'. Perhaps he omitted events on board the revenant's ship as it might have distracted the reader away from the focus of his tale, the poor ship carpenter and his children; perhaps he only knew a garbled conclusion. The events as relayed upto and including verse 26 do not suggest a conclusion as lame as the one in the seventeenth-century broadside.

As it happens, we can be fairly sure we 'know' who was the author of 'James Harris' a.k.a. 'A Warning to Married Women'. The initials L.P. are stamped at the end of the Roxburgh text of the ballad. Though these initials were not noted by Child, another of his assigned ballads, 'Robin Hood's Golden Prize' (Child 147), also bears these initials and draws the comment, "these would most naturally be the initials of the versifier."[20] *The Dictionary of National Biography* is more helpful. Under the entry for one Laurence Price, we find both a possible 'didactic purpose' and his most common moniker:

> **[Price] adapted his views to the times, and the godly puritan strain which he affected during the Commonwealth gave place to the utmost indecency after the Restoration ... He published much anonymously under the initials L.P.**[21]

'James Harris' was indeed first published as England was wilting under Cromwell's "godly puritan strain." Price has been identified as the 'author' of three Child ballads, 'Robin Hood's Golden Prize', 'The Famous Flower of Serving-Men' (Child 106), and 'James Harris'. The former two were both entered into the Stationers' Register in 1656, i.e. the year before 'James Harris'.

We now, needs must, come up against an essential contradiction in Child's 'definitive' collection of British popular ballads (and there can be little doubt that Child envisaged his collection as definitive). If Child believed these three ballads to be the work of a broadside hack then they should never have been included under his self-designated umbrella of 'popular' ballads which, he asserted, were anonymous "for the best of reasons." Child clearly did not consider that a ballad could become 'popular' by passing *into tradition* if it was as a broadside that it began life (otherwise the many British 'broadsides' like 'Pretty Polly', collected from America tradition, would all qualify). The broadsides Child did include, then, he must have believed had a popular tradition underlying them. And yet his own introduction to 'James Harris' damns him: "It does not seem necessary to posit a tradition behind [text] A."

In fact, there are good grounds for suspecting Price of doing precisely what inclusion in Child's work *should* imply, ransacking tradition for 'divers doggerel'. Price seems to have enjoyed some notoriety at the time for taking common lore and turning it into 'true tales', set to random popular tunes. The anonymous work *Mercurius Democritus*, published in April 1653, broke off from a particularly scurrilous tale to take a sideways swipe at our would-be bard:

> **More of this next week; because you shall then have the true relation in a Ballad, to the tune of the Seven Champions of the Pens in Smithfield, written by Laurenc[e] Price.**[22]

Price himself, rather than imprinting his usual moniker on his 1656 broadside 'A Wonderful Prophecy', noted instead that this work was "contrived into metre, by L.P."[23] Likewise, 'Robin Hood's Golden Prize', if we are to believe it is truly the work of Price, almost certainly predates its 1656 registration (Price was registering songs in the 1630s and was active as early as 1628). Certainly, "the kernel of the story," as Child observes in his notes to the song:

> **is an old tale, which we find represented in Pauli's Schimpf und Ernst, 1533 ... Three soldiers, out of service, meet the cellarer of a rich Benedictine cloister, who has a bag hanging at his saddle-bow, with four hundreds ducats in it. They ask for some money, for God's sake and good fellowship's. The cellarer answers that he has no money: there is nothing but letters in the bag. Then, since we all four are without money, they say, we will kneel down and pray for some. After a brief orison, the three jump up, search the bag, and find four hundred ducats. The cellarer offers them a handsome douceur, and says he had the money in the bag before; but to this they will give no credence. They give the monk his share of one hundred, and thank God devoutly for his grace.**[24]

45

This is exactly the tale told in 'Robin Hood's Golden Prize', presumably "contrived into metre, by L.P." Price may even have written the ballad in response to Martin Parker's 'A True Tale of Robin Hood' (Child 154), which was registered in February 1632. Parker and Price, the two most notorious broadside hacks of their day, were fierce rivals and Price may well have felt the need to 'compose' his own Robin Hood ballad (Child suffers rather badly from authors for his 'anonymous' Robin Hood ballads, two being composed by seventeenth century hacks and one - 'Robin Hood and the Pedlars' - being undoubtedly the work of notorious nineteenth century forger J. Payne Collier).

'The Famous Flower of Serving-Men', also registered in Price's name, provides an even more intriguing instance of possible debt. This time Child is of the opinion that, "The English broadside, *which may reasonably be believed to be formed upon a predecessor in the popular style* [my italics], has been held to have a common origin with the Scandinavian ballad, 'Maid and Stable Boy'."[25] Child also cites a Scottish ballad entitled 'Sweet Willie', collected by both Kinloch and Harris, as "derived from the broadside through recitation."[26] At no point does he entertain the possibility that the debt might be to, rather than from, 'Sweet Willie'.

The most damning evidence of an *a priori* source for this ballad is a musical one, found in Rimbault's *Musical Illustrations of Bishop Percy's Reliques [1850]*. He provides a tune for 'The Famous Flower of Serving-Men' which came "from an ancient lute book in the Editor's library, date about 1630."[27] This would pretty much preclude Price's authorship. Rimbault gives the tune a title - 'The Lady Turned Serving-Man' - though, as Bertrand Bronson observes, "one is seldom sure whether Rimbault's titles come from his mss. sources or from perceived resemblances between tunes known by various names."[28]

The tune in question derives from an Elizabethan air known as 'Callino Casturame'. It would be reasonable to assume that Rimbault had good grounds for assigning tune to title (Rimbault never felt compelled to draw upon tradition itself). One tune we can be reasonably sure does not correspond to the tune Rimbault had in mind for 'The Famous Flower of Serving-Men' is the one to which Price advised it sung: "Flora Farewell, Summertime, or, Love's Tide." As Bronson observes, "The tune, 'In Summertime' ... is not in LM [ballad-metre] as are all texts of the

46

present song," while 'Love's Tide', if Chappell is correct, is only "suited to 6-line anapaestic tetrameter stanzas."[29] 'The Famous Flower' is not such a beast.

Given that both 'The Famous Flower of Serving-Men', of which several Scottish variants had been collected by the end of the eighteenth century, and 'James Harris' were registered to Price, in 1656 and 1657 respectively, they may well suggest a common traditional source. Unfortunately we do not know where Price was during the latter part of the English Civil War. He ceased producing, or at least registering, his ballads between 1644 and 1656. One presumes he may have left London around 1644, when the victor in the conflict still remained a matter of doubt. Perhaps it was while stationed in the country that he came into contact with popular ditties like 'James Harris' and 'The Lady Turned Serving-Man'.

If Price was a surreptitious collector of traditional songs, it would appear, on the evidence of 'The Famous Flower of Serving-Men', that he was no musician. Originality in the tune department had never been one of Price's fortes. Though this in no way set him apart from his peers, it would have made rapid passage into tradition a tad problematic. The very inappropriateness of some of Price's assigned tunes suggests little thought was expended in their selection - Price intended 'his' songs to remain fixed on the page.

When it came to 'James Harris', or 'A Warning for Married Women', Price advised it sung, "to a West-country tune called 'The Fair Maid of Bristol', 'Bateman' or 'John True'." Perhaps the west-country setting simply suggested "a west-country tune." Unlikely. We should assume that Price had better cause for citing this particular song source. As it happens, the 'Bateman' referred to is not the famous ballad of 'Lord Bateman' but an early seventeenth century broadside sometimes known as 'Young Bateman' but more popularly known as 'A Warning For Fayre Maids', or 'A godly warning for all maidens'. The subject of this broadside, first registered in June 1603?:

It tells the story of an unnamed woman in Nottinghamshire who secretly exchanged vows of marriage with her lover, Young Bateman. Afterwards, however, she denied her vow and married a widower named

47

Jerman, 'Because he was of greater wealth/ and better of degree'. At this, Bateman warned her that she would never thenceforth be at peace and that he would have her, 'either now alive or dead,/ when I'm laid in grave'. He then hanged himself on the day of her wedding with Jerman. The bride subsequently fancied herself haunted by Bateman's ghost, which was constantly before her eyes, and which disturbed the night with cries and groans and reiterations of his determination to possess her. She was preserved just so long as she was pregnant with Jerman's child and consequently harbouring an innocent life, but, once it was born, Young Bateman's ghost came in the night and carried her away, never to be seen again.[30]

In this popular broadside - the final, moralizing verse of which opens this chapter - the spirit of young Bateman is variously referred to as 'ghost', 'spirit' or 'Fiend'. The tune to which this oft-reprinted broadside was directed to be sung was 'The Lady's Fall', otherwise known as 'Bateman' (later broadside reprints of 'James Harris' direct the song to be sung to 'The Lady's Fall'), while the curious disappearance of the lady in 'James Harris'("And since that time the woman-kind/Was never seen no more") seems almost a pastiche of the original 'Bateman' ("To what place no creature knew/Nor to this day can tell"). It would appear that the broadside's title, similarity of theme and even its specified tune were all aspects Price 'acquired' from this earlier broadside, and grafted onto a ballad in popular currency (the tune in question, 'The Lady's Fall', has not survived and therefore cannot take any appropriate test).

David Atkinson makes a very significant point, which he chooses not to develop, in his article 'Marriage & Retribution in "James Harris"':

> The two broadsides are similar in length and in theme, and both present their stories as factual, with names and places specified ... [but] the spirit does not quite engage the woman in conversation in 'A Warning for Maidens' as it does in 'A Warning for Married Women'.[31]

What we seem to have, with Price's 'James Harris', is a unique example of a broadside hack taking the story and 'dialogue' of a traditional ballad, which he had learnt/encountered by methods unknown, making it correspond in 'style' to a preexisting format, and a highly popular one at that, established by a 1603 broadside. The dialogue section of 'James

Harris' is the one stylistic element that sets it apart from 'A Warning for Maidens' because it was convenient for Price to utilize this section from the ballad he knew (though he still couldn't resist tampering with its language).

Ironically, the one rendition collected from English oral tradition that utilizes a verse *otherwise unique* to Price also betrays elements of Scottish traditional texts that could in no way have been directly inspired by Price's text. The penultimate verse of the text in question, collected c. 1896, has strong links to the final verse of Price's 'James Harris':

PRICE	MOORE
The children now are fatherless,	My infant Juan is left tonight,
And left without a guide,	Without father or mother;
But yet no doubt the heavenly powers	He's left tonight helpless, poor thing,
Will for them well provide.[32]	Left under God's mercy.

However, a 'full' recitation of this most curious rendition, collected by one Arthur William Moore from two Manx residents, and published in his 1896 collection, *Manx Ballads And Music,* illustrates the unlikelihood of even this rendition originating with Price's broadside (though it does appear that his melodramatic coda has herein been addended to a traditional text). Despite its omission from Bertrand Bronson's remarkably thorough *Traditional Tunes Of The Child Ballads*, Moore's text appears complete with tune (in 3/4 time, American versions tend to be in 4/4 or common time), and though the 'original' text is in Gaelic, under the title 'Yn Graider Jouylagh', Moore does provide an approximate translation:

1. Come with me, come with me now,
Come with me, my heart's love,
And I'll tell thee what came on me,
On the banks of Italy.

2. My ship now lies within the port,
Loaded with yellow gold,
All this I will bestow on thee:
Come with me, my heart's love.

3. I will clothe thee with beauteous silk,
Silk beauteous as can be,
If thou'lt come with me, my heart's love,
To the banks of Italy.

4. And costly shoes I'll give to thee,
Shoes made of yellow gold,
If thou'lt come with me, my heart's love,
To the banks of Italy.

5. As she was sitting on the deck,
List'ning to their sweet melody,
She was weeping and lamenting
For the infant Juan.

6. My infant Juan is left tonight,
Without father or mother;
He's left tonight helpless, poor thing,
Left under God's mercy.

7. O sit thee now close by my side,
Sit with me, my heart's love,
And I'll tell thee what came on us,
On the banks of Italy.[33]

The story, hopelessly corrupted in its transition to Gaelic, nevertheless
survived to the end of the nineteenth century (so much for William
Aytoun's, "No ballad can possibly be transmitted orally for centuries,
unless it has a clear intelligible story, with a main plot, to which all the
accessories tend"[34]). Perhaps surprisingly, given Celtic affiliations with
the world of spirits, the supernatural aspect has been sacrificed - along
with its sense - but the repeated references to "the banks of Italy," and
the allusions to "what came on us" there, unmistakeably ties the song to
Scottish oral tradition.

It would be quite a stretch to suggest that Price's song struck such a
chord that two sibling popular ballads - one English, one Scottish -
sprang from his parent-form (in fact, as we shall see, the song had

50

already developed two quite distinct identities by the time Price encountered it c.1650). Yet, by positing no tradition behind his A text, Child and his disciples require us to presume just such a rise and fall.

"The substance of the story" of 'James Harris' draws upon ten key motifs, all of which have cropped up in British tradition:
(i) the revenant nature of the 'man' is made apparent.
(ii) he is identified as James Harris.
(iii) the implication is that he has returned to her as a result of a vow made.
(iv) the passage of time since last they met is seven years.
(v) she is now married to a ship-carpenter, "a carpenter of great fame," and has three children.
(vi) James Harris could have married a king's daughter but did not break his vow.
(vii) she must now honour her vow by going with him.
(viii) she enquires as to his means of supporting her.
(ix) he assures her that he has "seven ships upon the sea."
(x) the ship in which she is to sail has sails "of finest silk" and a "mast of shining gold."

As it is, five of the motifs found in the 'James Harris' broadside fail to appear in the eighteenth century 'Distressed Ship-Carpenter' text yet *do* appear in 'traditionalist' renditions collected in Scotland in the early nineteenth century:

(i) the revenant nature of the 'man' is made apparent.
(ii) he is identified as James Harris.
(iii) the implication is that he has returned to her as a result of a vow made.
(iv) the passage of time since last they met is seven years.
(vii) she must now honour her vow by going with him.

Unfortunately, the traditional Scottish versions of 'The Dæmon Lover' in ESPB, culled from the great period of Scottish collecting - 1769, when David Herd's single volume *Ancient & Modern Scots Songs* first appeared, to 1830, by which time the likes of Burns, Jamieson, Pinkerton, Kinloch, Sharpe, Motherwell, Scott and Buchan had all gathered their material - amount to a mere half a dozen, of which just three (Buchan, Motherwell [E] and Scott) tell a full tale. These are slim pickings indeed.

Child assigns these six Scottish versions accordingly:
C. 'James Herries', from Buchan's Ballads of the North of Scotland I, 214. [26 verses]
D. 'The Carpenter's Wife', George Kinloch's ms., I, 297. [9 verses].
E. 'The Dæmon Lover', William Motherwell's ms., p.97. [18 verses].
F. 'The Dæmon Lover', Scott's Minstrelsy, II, 427. [15 verses].
G. 'The Dæmon Lover', Motherwell's Minstrelsy, p.93. [9 verses].
H. 'The Banks of Italy', Christie, Traditional Ballad Airs, I, 138 [2 verses]
plus, as an appendix to F, six verses sung by Walter Grieve paraphrased by William Laidlaw in a letter to Walter Scott, dated January 3, 1803.

None of these versions gives us an archetypal template, nor can they be comfortably reconciled into a singular form. As such, deciding which Scottish text/s may have the deepest core of tradition, we must first examine the number of parallels with Price's 'James Harris' broadside, presupposing - as I do - that verses 17-26 of Price derive from tradition, and probably a Scottish one at that.

Of course, one possible textual clue that it is a Scottish tradition is the name of the revenant itself, James Harris. Surely such a name points a rigid digit north of the border. It does not strike me as the sort of name that a seventeenth century blackletter wordsmith would light upon as the name of a West Country youth "press'd to sea." Rather, I suspect, Price has retained the name from the traditional song he appropriated, the ghost identifying himself accordingly in verse seventeen, as the former lovers' dialogue begins. James would lang remain the favourite name of Scottish kings. As to the Scottish credentials of the name Harris, Buchan had this to say in the notes to his published version:

> James Herries was a branch of the Anglo-Norman family of Heriz, who came to Scotland during the age of David. It is more than probable that the same William de Heriz, who appears to have attached himself to David I, and his son Henry, may have settled in Scotland. The representative of all those Herizes, Sir Herbert, obtained the title of Lord Herries of Terregles in 1493. From this stock are sprung the several families of Herris in Scotland.[35]

If the tale itself - and ten verses of dialogue - derived from tradition, then Price's verses represent our best clue as to what that tradition might have been in the early seventeenth century. However, locating a more 'traditionalist' version of our tale requires another fast-forward, to the windswept climes of early nineteenth century Aberdeenshire, and the oft-disparaged endeavours of one of its native sons, Peter Buchan.

(iv) The Besmirching of Peter Buchan.

That Mr. Buchan has not published his ballads with that scrupulous accuracy, that strict and verbal adherence to the popular tradition, as might be wished, and which may now be demanded, we are ready to confess; but he has certainly done no worse in that respect than all the ballad editors of England and Scotland, with the exceptions of Mr. Ritson, Mr. Jamieson, and perhaps one or two more. His merits in preservation of the old Scottish folklore are so great, that he certainly ought to be treated in a less slighting manner than has been the case. - Svend Grundtvig.[1]

Though Buchan's is the Scottish version with the closest correspondence to the 'James Harris' broadside, his own reputation as an honest, methodical collector has repeatedly been queried by Child and other literary scholars like T.F. Henderson, who shared Child's distaste for field-collecting. One must therefore first rehabilitate Buchan, before comparing his text with his contemporaries' - Scott, Motherwell and Kinloch - and, indeed, the two English broadsides, hopefully establishing the 'authenticity' of what is, on the face of it, our best and, at twenty-six verses, our longest traditional text for 'The Dæmon Lover'.

Peter Buchan has certainly had extraordinarily bad press from the sons of Ritson. Yet he is, in many ways, the most important of all nineteenth century Scottish ballad collectors. Between 1816 and 1838, Buchan collected some 577 songs and ballads - including 76 rather high-kilted items contained in a private ms. entitled *Secret Songs Of Silence,* at a time when such catholic tastes in collecting continued to be frowned upon by the literati - making him the most prodigious field-collector of his time. His work certainly seems to have excited contemporary ballad scholars. Motherwell craved permission to utilize some of Buchan's texts in his own ballad collection. Letters from the likes of Robert Jamieson, C.K. Sharpe and Walter Scott rhapsodized about Buchan's first manuscript, the product of his first eleven years of collecting, from which came *Ancient Ballads & Songs From The North Of Scotland*, published in 1828. Scott enthused about the collection to Buchan himself and in an August 1827 entry in his journal, wrote:

> **He has been very successful [in his collecting], for they are obviously genuine, and many of them very curious ... It is a great pity that few of these ballads are historical, almost all being of the romantic cast. They certainly ought to be preserved, after striking out one or two which have been sophisticated, I suppose, by Mr. Buchan himself, which are easily distinguishable from the genuine ballads.[2]**

Writing privately to ballad authority C.K. Sharpe, Scott also provided a most backhanded compliment when he suggested that Buchan himself was quite incapable of convincing forgery:

> **His collection is very curious, and, two or three pieces excepted, in general genuine. Indeed, the man does not seem capable of supplying their want of authenticity by any tolerable degree of genius. I scarce know anything as easily discovered as the piecing and patching of an old ballad, the darns in a silk stocking are not more manifest.[3]**

Sharpe's own correspondence with Buchan betrays no concerns about the ballads' legitimacy, indeed he is credited with "revising the proof-sheets" of Buchan's 1828 collection. And yet Child treated Buchan's texts with a barely-disguised contempt. In a remarkable correspondence between Child and his Danish peer, Svend Grundtvig, leading upto the publication of *English & Scottish Popular Ballads*, Grundtvig was repeatedly required to puncture Child's delusion that popular ballads were composed by "a class of people" (as close as Child was prepared to come to accepting the 'communal origins' theory championed by the likes of Herder, Grimm &c.). When the ballads in Buchan's 1828 collection came under Child's gavel, he actually accused Buchan of wholesale forgery:

> **From the internal evidence, the extraordinary vulgarity, especially, of many of his ballads, I should think that he must have tampered very extensively with his originals, if even he did not invent out and out.[4]**

Grundtvig patiently pointed out that many ballads unique to Buchan's collection had Danish parallels to which Buchan himself could not have had reference. He then reminded Child of the dangers of preconceiving the character of popular ballads:

What you term the 'vulgarity' of the Buchan texts is to me the best proof of their material authenticity ... In the recent traditions of the common country people (peasantry) the old ballad cannot always appear in a stately and knightly form and apparel, but must in many instances exhibit the traces of a long dwelling in humble company. And besides, very often what now to delicate eyes and ears may seem 'vulgar', is in fact the old stamp, retaining the features and phrases of the higher classes in the middle ages. For the chivalry in reality was by no means so refined and sentimental as it appears in modern romance ... Let us have the old national ballads as antique and genuine as possible ... but in their own clothes, and be judged by their own standard.[5]

Child continued to betray a fixed mindset - *popular ballads will conform to my template or henceforth ne'er ballads be* - in his next letter to Grundtvig:

[On] the subject of Buchan's forgeries, his deviations from all other versions are very remarkable, not merely in their range, but in their kind, and they are all of one sort. They exhibit an artificial vulgarity, it seems to me, and as I have said, there is no variety to this, which makes me fear that it comes from a man and not from a class of people. How is it that Kinloch's ballads, which were also gathered in the North of Scotland, and which are given without the slightest editorial interference, show nothing of the kind? The vulgarity that I mean consists of a tame, mean, unreal style of expression, far from *volksmassig*. I do not find this in any other ballads.[6]

It is significant that Child should use a term (*volksmassig*) from the German school of Metaphysics to quosh Buchan's decidedly unmetaphysical texts. Child did eventually incorporate most of Buchan's ballad-texts into *English & Scottish Popular Ballads*, though rarely assigning them pole position (the 'A' text), and he continued to reserve a most unacademic turn of phrase for items unique to Buchan, e.g. 'The White Fisher': "We need not trouble ourselves much to make these counterfeits reasonable. Those who utter them rely confidently upon our taking folly and jargon as the marks of genuineness."[7] Gavin Greig's post-Child excavations of the same territory as Buchan uncovered an excellent text of 'The White Fisher' (as did the American James Carpenter), proving Buchan in this instance to be neither a falsifier nor a fraud.

56

William Walker - who corresponded with Child in the latter stages of *English & Scottish Popular Ballads*, endeavouring to broker a deal between Buchan's nephew and Harvard University for Buchan's original ballad ms. - also spent much time trying to make Child see the error of his ways. Walker should take some of the credit for so many Buchan ballads appearing in Child's final two volumes. Walker published a thorough overview of Buchan's work, *Peter Buchan & Other Papers*, in 1915, in which he pertinently concluded:

> **The main difference between Buchan's ballads and those of some other collectors resolves itself into the personal difference in mental equipment and taste between them as editors. That Buchan touched up and eked out some of the material he gathered - as more or less all ballad editors of his time did - we have no doubt. That these touches and ekes were bound to be wooden, or something worse, is just what one would expect from his lack of literary taste, and poetic outlook. Yet on the whole, he did not work over the defects of his records, but rather spliced them, so that one can get in Buchan's text, nearer to what really lived on the lips of his generation of traditional balladry, than in that of any other collector we know.[8]**

And that is the crux of the matter, that "in Buchan's text [we get] nearer to what really lived on the lips of his generation of traditional balladry," not filtered through the literary siv of a Scott or a Percy.

There is certainly no evidence that Buchan perpetrated 'fake' traditional texts, nor that he might be, in Scott's choice phrase, "capable of supplying their want of authenticity." Privately Buchan was fiercely critical of those whose "disagreeable and disgusting emendations and interpolations [are] so frequently met with in [ballad collections]."[9] In correspondence with fellow ballad-collector William Motherwell, Buchan on one occasion provided him with both a version of 'Waly, Waly' and an insight into his own methodology:

> **In this parcel ... there is a copy of 'False Colin' or 'Waly, Waly', collated with [sic] two versions, the one from the recitation of my blind minstrel [James Rankin], and the other from an old woman. The difference between them is not very material; but as I am a sworn foe of emendations etc. I would not substitute a single word from Ramsay['s Tea-Table**

Miscellany], and you have it in its original purity, with all its imperfections.[10]

Clearly, then, Buchan had no qualms about collating two versions collected from tradition into a single 'publishable' text. However, he also disdained the printed texts of known "emenders and interpolators." It is in this light that Buchan's text of 'James Herries' should perhaps be read. Even with its unique introduction and commonplace conclusion, it comes across like the product of one particular stream of tradition:

1. O are ye my father? Or are ye my mother?
Or are ye my brother John?
Or are ye James Herries, my first true-love,
Come back to Scotland again?

2. I am not your father, I am not your mother,
Nor am I your brother John;
But I'm James Herries, your first true-love,
Come back to Scotland again.

3. Awa, awa, ye former lover,
Had far awa frae me!
For now I am another man's wife
Ye'll ne'er see joy o me.

4. Had I kent that ere I came here,
I ne'er had come to thee;
For I might hae married the king's daughter,
Sae fain she woud had me.

5. I despised the crown o' gold,
The yellow silk also,
And I am come to my true-love,
But with me she'll not go.

6. My husband he is a carpenter,
Makes his bread on dry land,
And I hae born him a young son;
Wi' you I will not gang.

7. You must forsake your dear husband,
Your little young son also,
Wi' me to sail the raging seas,
Where the stormy winds do blow.

8. O what hae you to keep me wi',
If I should with you go,
If I'd forsake my dear husband,
My little young son also?

9. See ye not yon seven pretty ships?
The eighth brought me to land,
With merchandize and mariners,
And wealth in every hand.

10. She turnd her round upon the shore
Her love's ships to behold;
Their topmasts and their mainyards
Were coverd o'er wi' gold.

11. Then she's gane to her little young son,
And kissd him cheek and chin;

Sae has she to her sleeping husband,
And dune the same to him.

12. O sleep ye, wake ye, my husband?
I wish ye wake in time!
I wouldna for ten thousand pounds
This night ye knew my mind.

13. She's drawn the slippers on her feet,
Were coverd o'er wi' gold,
Well lined within wi' velvet fine,
To had her frae the cold.

14. She hadna sailed upon the sea
A league but barely three
Till she minded on her dear husband,
Her little young son tee.

15. O gin I were at land again,
At land where I would be,
The woman ne'er should bear the son
Should gar me sail the sea.

16. O hold your tongue, my sprightly flower,
Let a' your mourning be;
I'll show you how the lilies grow
On the banks o' Italy.

17. She hadna sailed on the sea
A day but barely ane
Till the thoughts o' grief came in her mind,
And she langd for to be hame.

18. O gentle death, come cut my breath,

I may be dead ere morn!
I may be buried in Scottish ground,
Where I was bred and born!

19. O hold your tongue, my lily leesome thing,
Let a' your mourning be;
But for a while we'll stay at Rose Isle,
Then see a far countrie.

20. Ye'se ne'er be buried in Scottish ground,
Nor land ye's nae mair see;
I brought you away to punish you
For the breaking your vows to me.

21. I said ye should see the lilies grow
On the banks o' Italy;
But I'll let you see the fishes swim,
In the bottom o' the sea.

22. He reached his hand to the topmast,
Made a' the sails gae down,
And in the twinkling o' an e'e
Baith ship and crew did drown.

23. The fatal flight o' this wretched maid
Did reach her ain countrie;
Her husband then distracted ran,
And this lament made he:

24. O wae be to the ship, the ship,
And wae be to the sea,
And wae be to the mariners
Took Jeanie Douglas frae me!

25. O bonny, bonny was my love,

A pleasure to behold;
The very hair o' my love's head
Was like the threads o' gold.

26. O bonny was her cheek, her cheek,
And bonny was her chin,
And bonny was the bride she was,
The day she was made mine![11]

Buchan's one true crime against tradition is that he never cited his sources nor preserved his notes. As such, 'James Herries', like Price's 'James Harris', has come down to us only as printed. Though there are three Buchan manuscripts, two at Harvard, one at the British Museum - which between them appear to comprise every song he collected around Aberdeenshire - the manuscripts in question only provide 'clean' copies of the songs, not a verbatim record of what he took down from reciters.

In one sense at least, then, Child was entitled to be suspicious - Buchan's texts tend to be so much more complete than any of his contemporaries. Repetitions and corruptions were often incorporated, whatever their relevance to the text. The last two verses of 'James Herries' - which clearly have no connection with the song - would have been deleted in the interests of sense by a more literary editor. Likewise, the second couplet in verse 19 ("But for a while/ we'll stay at Rose Isle...") serves no obvious purpose and breaks the momentum. Perhaps verses 19 and 20 originally formed a single verse of triple rhyming-couplets, something found in certain medieval ballads:

> O hold your tongue, my lily leesome thing,
> Let a' your mourning be;
> Ye'se ne'er be buried in Scottish ground,
> Nor land ye's nae mair see;
> I brought you away to punish you
> For the breaking [of] your vows to me.

The six-line stanza, where it is encountered, tends to signpost a significant shift in tone, as it would here. Buchan's verse 18 should also perhaps reverse couplets, thus retaining the internal rhyming-line in its traditional slot, i.e.

> May I be buried in Scottish ground,
> Where I was bred and born,
> O gentle death, come cut my breath, [Artificial vulgarity?!]
> I may be dead ere morn.

The incongruous intrusions seem merely to confirm that Buchan incorporated all he took down, the logical *and* the nonsensical. He did not include the 'hills of heaven' verses already published in Scott, despite the fact that he made great play in his introduction of the fact that he had found a "complete" text for 'James Herries'. If he was the literary forger he was reputed to be he would surely have added these verses in the obvious place, between verses 21 and 22, making for an even more 'complete' text. They are not there because he evidently did not encounter them on his travels.

Some corroboration for the authenticity of the Buchan 'James Herries' is provided by a sadly-incomplete text, collected by Gavin Greig in the same area as much of Buchan's collecting, in the year 1907. Greig's version, collected from Alexander & Ms. Annie Robb, runs to only five and a half verses but what there is parallels Buchan's very nicely:

> 1. She's ta'en her young son in her arms, [Buchan 11]
> And gi'en him kisses three,
> And she bade adieu to auld Scotland,
> And awa wi' you I'll gae.
>
> 2. She hadna sailed a week, a week, [Buchan 17]
> A week but barely three,
> When she began to mind on her man,
> And her bonnie young son tee.
>
> 3. Oh, haud your tongue, my dear, he said, [Buchan 16]
> Oh, haud your tongue, said he,
> And I'll lat ye see the bonnie lilies grow
> On the banks o' Italy.
>
> 4. They hadna sailed a week, a week,

A week but barely three,
Till dark and rainy grew the day,
And raging grew the sea.

5. ...
And I'll lat ye see the white fish swim [Buchan 21]
On the banks o' Littertie.

6. He turned roon his bonnie ship [Buchan 22]
Wi' her topmast to the win';
And all her seven sails did sink,
And was never seen again.[12]

Though neither Buchan nor Greig has any hills of heaven and hell, they both endow our revenant with the preternatural ability to sink the ship with a wave of his hand, something beyond the powers of your common or garden ghost. The suspicion remains that our James Harris may be something even more disturbing than "a ghost come back from out in the sea."

(v) Saw Ye My Father?

Each singer is confident that his own [version] is the right one, but the collector soon learns that there is no right, and they have all to be written. And then he becomes possessed of a family whose relationship it is hard or even impossible to trace. He will have twin sisters hardly distinguishable from each other, and parents and offspring plainly enough declared; but oftener he will have a crowd of relations whose connection shades off into all degrees, while he will also discover intermarriages ... of the most extraordinary kind. - J.B. Duncan.[1]

There are just three texts which name the revenant at the heart of our tale: the Price broadside of 1657; Peter Buchan's text, published in 1828; and the Sullivan text collected by Helen Hartness Flanders in Vermont in 1932. However, if we accept 'George Allis' as a plausible phonetic corruption of the name, then all agree on 'James Harris'. Of the Scottish oral versions, Buchan's provides the largest number of 'traditional' elements. Buchan collected in the hillocks surrounding Peterhead, 45 miles north-east of Aberdeen - as far removed from the urban world of Laurence Price as a nineteenth-century mainlander could be. And yet of verses 17-26 in the broadside, just verse 19 and the second couplet in verse 23 do not find a correspondence in Buchan, while four of the five 'traditional' motifs evident in the 17th century broadside - yet absent from its eighteenth century equivalent - are contained in Buchan:
(i) the revenant nature of the 'man' is made apparent.
(ii) he is identified as James Harris.
(iii) the implication is that he has returned to her as a result of a vow made.
(vii) she must now honour her vow by going with him.

Though s/he does not specify the passage of time elapsed, Buchan's source assuredly makes the breaking of her vows the motive for James Harris's posthumous return:

> Ye'se ne'er be buried in Scottish ground,
> Nor land ye's nae mair see;
> I brought you away to punish you

> For the breaking [of] your vows to me.[2]

Likewise - in verse 23 of the broadside - Price reiterates the broken vow as the reason for his return:

> I will forgive thee what is past,
> If thou wilt with me go.[3]

Evidently the 'broken vows' had been the 'veritable crux' as far back as the mid-seventeenth century.

On the other hand, could not the revenant element be something Price appropriated from 'Young Bateman', rather than the traditional original of 'James Harris'? Not if, as it would appear, Price took the prosaic route of constructing his history of the doomed couple entirely from hints in the traditional song. He makes James Harris's revenant nature explicit in verses 16-17, verses without parallel in any traditional text. And yet Buchan manages what no other 'extant' rendition achieves - he makes the identity of the ghost overt without taking Price's prosaic route, utilizing opening verses unique to his version of 'The Dæmon Lover', though referential to at least one other Scottish revenant ballad:

> O are ye my father? Or are ye my mother?
> Or are ye my brother John?
> Or are ye James Herries, my first true-love,
> Come back to Scotland again?
>
> I am not your father, I am not your mother,
> Nor am I your brother John;
> But I'm James Herries, your first true-love,
> Come back to Scotland again.[4]

A ballad of no fixed denomination, entitled 'The Grey Cock', first published by David Herd in 1769, also concerns itself with the appearance of a loved one late at night, who turns out to be the spirit of a former lover. When the cock crows the day, he must return to his grave. Its 1769 form ran to just four verses:

> O saw ye my father, or saw ye my mother,

Or saw ye my true love John
I saw not your Father, I saw not your Mother,
But I saw your true love John.

Up Johny rose, and to the door he goes,
And gently tirled the pin;
The lassie taking tent unto the door she went,
And she opend and let him in.

Flee, flee up, my bonny grey cock,
And craw whan it is day;
Your neck shall be like the bonny beaten gold,
And your wings of the silver grey.

The cock prov'd false, and untrue he was,
For he crew an hour o'er soon;
The lassie thought it day when she sent her love away,
And it was but a blink of the moon.[5]

Only by inference - and knowledge of other revenant ballads - has 'The Grey Cock' been entered into the revenant ballad canon. Even a further three verses uncovered by Herd before his second edition in 1776 "do [little] more than bridge the most palpable gaps in the readiest way"[6] and the deathly identity of Johny has had to remain implicit at best. The song was known to James Johnson, who gave it a tune (and a new title, 'Saw Ye My Father') in his 1787 *Scots Musical Museum*, as well as featuring in the St. Clair ms. (c. 1770s), again in four-verse form, suggesting that this curiously mangled ballad enjoyed some popular currency in the mid-eighteenth century. However, 'The Grey Cock' does not appear to have any established antique provenance. If there was a debt *from* 'The Grey Cock' *to* 'James Herries' it would almost certainly have been a modern interpolation (to Buchan, that is).

In fact 'The Grey Cock' appears to be little more than a melange of revenant 'forms' or conventions. The last two verses, it has been confidently asserted, derive from an Irish folk song entitled 'The Lover's Ghost', in which the revenant makes his nature explicit at song's end, with the admission that:

"The clay is my bed, my dearest dear," he said,
"The shroud is my white holland sheet;
The worms and the creeping things are my waiting maids,
To wait on me whilst I am asleep."[7]

The 'saw ye my father' verse does not appear in any other 'Lover's Ghost' hybrid, of which there have been few, mostly located in Nova Scotia and Newfoundland. Despite this, attempts have been made to entwine 'Lover's Ghost' and 'The Grey Cock' under the Child umbrella. The dangers of attempting to discern original from imitation in folksong are appositely illustrated by the passage through balladry of these particular verses. Though Phillips Barry has asserted that the Irish ballad, 'The Lover's Ghost', "must stand as the original of 'The Grey Cock',"[8] Bronson takes pains to correct Barry, reminding us that the likely 'source' for *all* the verses - the cock's crow, the 'saw ye my father' and the-grave-is-my-bed - is a far more obviously antique receptacle of Scottish revenant lore:

> Without pausing to cavil about the word 'original', it seems more in keeping with the evidence to regard 'The Lover's Ghost' as a 'variety' (Child's word) of 'Sweet William's Ghost', and to consider the latter as the true parent.[9]

The essential motif in the tale of Sweet William is that "the dead lover returns [at night] to ask back his unfulfilled troth-plight." The lady, uncertain who has come to her door, asks:

Are ye my father, the king? she says,
Or are ye my brother John?
Or are you my true-love, Sweet William,
From England newly come?

I'm not your father, the king, he says,
No, no, nor your brother John;
But I'm your true love, Sweet William,
From England that's newly come.[10]

A relationship between 'The Dæmon Lover' and 'Sweet William's Ghost' is far more likely than with 'The Grey Cock'. Bronson even suggests that "there may be a connection"[11] with the tunes themselves. Like 'James Herries', the ballad revolves around a vow to marry, lying between the recently-dead and the living. Once again, the soul of the revenant cannot rest until the matter is resolved. However, in this case the lady has done no wrong and the revenant must simply beg for the return of his troth, eventually being forced to reveal his true nature:

> "O Lady Marjory, Lady Marjory,
> For faith and charitie,
> Will you give me my faith and troth,
> That I gave once to thee?"

> "O your faith and troth I'll not give thee,
> No, no, that will not I,
> Until I get one kiss of your ruby lips,
> And in my arms you come [lye]."

> "My lips they are so bitter, he says,
> My breath it is so strong,
> If you get one kiss of my ruby lips,
> Your days will not be long."[12]

The final verse refers to a longstanding belief among 'der volk' that kissing the dead on the lips would spell imminent doom. It is significant that in 'Sweet William's Ghost' the identity of the revenant is not in doubt, largely because he is required to reveal himself. However, methinks I spy the thumbprint of some blackletter hack in an opening verse that appears in some variants:

> There came a ghost to Margret's door,
> With many a grievous groan,
> And ay he tirled at the pin,
> But answer made she none.[13]

'Sweet William's Ghost' does not require reference to any other ballad to determine the significance of its opening verses. Buchan's 'James Herries' *presupposes* awareness *from its audience* that such an opening bespeaks a revenant returning to a former love. Though it is tempting to interpret these verses as simply an interpolation from 'Sweet William's

Ghost' that have attached themselves to a 'typically-corrupt' Buchan text, external evidence suggests this is not one of Buchan's badly-spliced constructs but probably represents authentic tradition. The clues in question are buried within the other two extant variants of what we might call the 'James Harris' strain, i.e. the 'James Harris' broadside and the 'George Allis' fragment. In neither case is the familiar opening riposte, "Well met, well met...," encountered, nor indeed appropriate.

Whereas Laurence Price chose to construct his own backdrop to the lovers' encounter, Ms. Sullivan recalled no opening verses at all. However, Ms. Sullivan did recall the circumstances of their meeting, that "she lay asleep and his ghost came to her." In no way can such a scenario be reconciled with the conventional 'Ship Carpenter' opening. It self-evidently accords with the 'revenant' opening in Buchan and, indeed, 'Sweet William's Ghost'. Likewise, in 'James Harris' our spirit explictly returns at night, frightening the young lady until he identifies himself in a way akin to Buchan:

PRICE	BUCHAN
'James Harris is my name,' quoth he, Whom thou didst love so dear.	I'm James Herries, your first true-love, Come back to Scotland again.

Though 'James Herries' draws on the convention, it cannot have originated it. Yet it strikes me as equally dangerous to assume that the two verses in question originated with 'Sweet William's Ghost'. How these conventions arose remains shrouded in as much mystery as the origins of balladry itself. Milmam Parry seems to have conceived the most logical premise back in 1932:

> **When one singer ... has hit upon a phrase which is pleasing and easily used, other singers will hear it, and then, when faced at the same point in the [song] with the need of expressing the same idea, they will recall it and use it. If the phrase is so good poetically and so useful metrically that it becomes in time the one best way to express a certain idea in a given length of the verse, and *as such is passed on from one generation of poets to another,* it has won a place for itself in the oral diction as a formula.[14]**

68

Unfortunately, Parry's notion, bound up as it is with the birth of the oral-formulaic school, has taken on unfortunate connotations. If a ballad formula is "a group of words which is regularly employed under the same metrical conditions to express a given essential idea,"[15] then our convention is just such a formula. But the convention in question cannot have been essentially oral-formulaic in conceit (i.e. a metrical tool used spontaneously in performance when seeking "to express a given essential idea," a practise I am not convinced was ever an important part of the creative ballad tradition). Its intent, I believe, was to establish a context for the singer's audience. No action is attendant upon its use, it is a coded 'incipit', i.e. a formulaic opening in early revenant ballads - one that may or may not have originated with an extant ballad - the 'import' of which was gradually forgotten as the audience lost contact with the wellspring from which these ballads sprung, so that "a stylistic feature that once had a specific function ...[later] persist[ed] as a mere habit or an empty rhetorical flourish."[16]

The 'James Harris' strain of 'The Dæmon Lover' originally must have contained lines that made the revenant's identity explicit to the audience since a great deal of the underlying tension in the ballad derives from the audience's awareness of the dangers the woman in the song 'willingly' embraces. Likewise, in 'Sweet William's Ghost' the audience must know of the revenant's identity *before* he reveals it to his love.

If so, the convention in question suggests a time when singer and audience were as one, and popular balladry itself was capable of containing both narrative and 'supra-narrative' elements - without "the supra-narrative function [being] arbitrarily separated from the narrative function."[17] In this instance the narrative function is to introduce the two central characters, their former relationship and the time of the former lover's return. The supra-narrative function is to make the audience aware that the former lover is no mere mortal, but a revenant returned from the grave. This suggests a degree of conceptual sophistication on the part of both singer AND audience. It also suggests a set of balladic conventions already maleable to the composers of ballads, "supra-narrative functions ... hav[ing] grown out of their narrative content, by the frequent employment in the same context."[18]

If 'James Harris' has a pedigree extending some way back from Price, and the Buchan opening is referential to an ancient convention also reflected in 'Sweet William's Ghost', then we are required to suppose that 'Sweet William's Ghost' shared a concurrent popularity in Scotland. The ballad, separated from 'The Distressed Ship-Carpenter' in *A Collection Of Diverting Songs* by only a few pages, was clearly in popular currency at the beginning of the eighteenth century, appearing just three years later in the fourth edition of Allan Ramsay's *Tea-Table Miscellany*.

One version of 'Sweet William's Ghost' adds a further motif common to Scottish variants of 'James Harris', and again it appears to be bound up with popular revenant lore at a time, and among a people, beyond our ken. In Jamieson's version (Child F), the song opens with Lady Margaret, having mourned for seven years over her former lover, intending to throw herself over the castle wall:

> When seven years were come and gane,
> Lady Margaret she thought lang;
> And she is up to the hichest tower,
> By the lee licht o the moon.
>
> She was lookin o'er her castle high,
> To see what she might fa',
> And there she saw a grieved ghost,
> Comin' waukin' o'er the wa'.[19]

Though Buchan's 'James Herries' provides no term for the ghost's return, his is the exception amongst Scottish texts. Even in our seventeenth century broadside, verse 18 - one of the verses to smack of traditional probity - refers overtly to the passage of time since last they met - seven years. Kinloch, Motherwell and Scott all agree:

> O whare hae ye been, my dearest dear,
> These seven lang years and more?
> O I am come to seek my former vows,
> That ye promised me before.[20]

Child seems to miss its possible significance, commenting, "what is meant in stanza 18 by his travelling seven years, it is not easy to understand." Yet the span of seven years clearly once had an import now lost. Lowry Charles Wimberly, in *Folklore In English & Scottish Ballads*, notes its frequency in British ballads:

> **Lady Margaret's dead lover returns after 'seven years were come and gane', as does also the demon-lover in 'James Harris'. To collate two old pieces, 'The Cruel Mother' and 'The Maid and the Palmer', which instance the belief in transmigration, a wicked mother must perform a series of seven-year penances by becoming a bird, a fish, a church bell, a stone or a porter in hell ... Though not so popular as three, the number seven occurs with great frequency in the British ballads - a noteworthy point in view of the fact that it is said not to be a favourite number in England. As regards certain ballad incidents it is probably of mystical significance.[21]**

That the "mystical significance" is of some antiquity, and seems to relate in some way to Lucifer's kingdom, is borne out by the ballads in which it is a key motif. In the fifteenth century 'Tam Lin' seven years is the span of time when the Queen of the Fairies must pay a tithe to Hell. 'The Maid and the Palmer', which appears in our best source of pre-seventeenth century ballads, the Percy folio, but, like 'The Dæmon Lover', was not collected in Scotland until the early nineteenth century, also relates a series of seven-year sentences in hell:

> Penance I can give thee none,
> But seven yeere to be a stepping-stone.
>
> Other seven a clapper in a bell,
> Other seven to lead an ape in hell..[22]

As such, it seems to me that neither Buchan nor Price have the entire 'authentic' opening to 'James Herries'. In its original form, I surmise, the ghost's identity must have been evident to the audience but not the lady; the passage of seven years would have been clearly stated (and, equally importantly, its significance understood by the audience); and common ground agreed as to the solemnity of vows in the sight of God.

For a Buchan-like text, *of Scottish origin*, to have interacted with the English broadside form - first around 1650 and then around 1720 -

surviving in southern English oral tradition into the late nineteenth century, suggests a song that must have thrived in British tradition throughout the seventeenth and into the eighteenth century. However, the Buchan strain must have interacted with another British strain, and interacted with it before its passage to America, if we are to reconcile all the motifs in American tradition with a parent oral tradition. Evidence of this interaction is suggested by another text collected in Aberdeenshire, one contemporaneous with Buchan, but absent from Child.

(vi) Scott of Glenbuchat.

The ballads are not what they would have been two hundred years ago, but ... I have undertaken to make a [brocade] of every Rag the wild Muse ever wore. - Francis J. Child.[1]

English & Scottish Popular Ballads (1882-98) was a direct result of the nagging dissatisfaction Child felt for an earlier collection, *English & Scottish Ballads* (1857-59), that he had agreed to edit as part of a popular anthology series in eight slim volumes. In the earlier collection, Child had worked entirely from printed sources - the published collections of Percy, Scott, Jamieson, Motherwell, Buchan and Kinloch providing the bulk of the texts. However, Child knew as well as anyone that even the best of these editors had taken liberties with their material and decided that, given the chance again, his "chief duty [would] be to give all the known texts and to give them pure."[2]

It would take Child another twenty-five years to reel in the manuscripts necessary to commence his *magnum opus* and, even upto his final months (Child died on September 11, 1896) he was "pursu[ing] a manuscript when I get a scent of one, with as much tenacity as time has left me capable of."[3] Thanks to William Walker, Buchan's original manuscript collection of ballads (1816-27) arrived that summer, in time for Child to peruse it but not use it (he had been working from a later composite ms. he found in the British Museum for the previous twenty-two years).

Remarkably few manuscripts *from oral tradition* eluded the diligent scholar. A manuscript compiled by Elizabeth St. Clair in the 1770s, "supposed to contain Songs"[4], turned out to have some sixteen Child ballads among its 204 ditties when eventually purchased in auction by Child's most indefatigible Scottish helper, William MacMath, shortly after his death. Child was able to call upon just two St. Clair texts, copied from her ms. into his own by C.K. Sharpe. Of Andrew Crawfurd's collection of ballads and songs - compiled between 1826 and 1828, and recently published in two volumes by the Scottish Text Society and containing around eighty Scottish popular ballad variants - Child had access to just twenty-one ballad-texts, those items Motherwell integrated into his own ballad ms.

In terms of late eighteenth and early nineteenth century Scottish ballad texts, that would appear to be it were it not for four volumes of ballads collected by a Reverend Scott in a remote parish near Aberdeen, some time before 1818, comprising the so-called 'Glenbuchat ms.' Though Child seems to have been wholly unaware of the existence of Scott's collection, a reference to the manuscript does appear in William Stenhouse's 1853 edition of *The Scots Musical Museum*, an edition Child cited in his bibliography. In his additional notes to Burns' 'Lady Mary Ann', Stenhouse comments that the song:

> **was modelled by Burns from a fragment of an anicent ballad, entitled 'Craigton's Growing' ['Young Craigston' a.k.a. 'Young But Daily Growin'], still preserved in a manuscript collection of Ancient Scottish Ballads, in the possession of the Rev. Robert Scott, minister of the parish of Glenbucket. Several old ballads, which have hitherto been considered as lost, appear in this collection.[5]**

By the time Child began work on ESPB, both Stenhouse and Scott had died and this manuscript of "several old ballads" was forgotten - until 1949, that is, when George Davidson, a curator at Aberdeen University, handed the ms. over to the university archives, having acquired it from the great-granddaughter of Robert Scott during the war. There are just sixty-seven items in the manuscript, yet it contains sixty-one variants of some fifty-eight Child ballads.

That such a store of Scottish ballads could be collected from a parish whose population, in the years Scott collected, rose from 443 to 479, might not beggar belief but certainly "adds powerful testimony to the density and strength of [this particular] regional tradition."[6] That almost nothing is known about Scott's methodology, or the timescale his collecting occupied, makes for another frustrating addendum to the dark areas Child's Scottish sources are wont to inhabit. That Scott's collection was wholly devoted to ballads, indeed solely to the traditional variety of ballad, suggests that Scott was highly selective in his collecting, and that his interest must have been essentially literary (there are no tunes in the ms.). Scott was surely one of those inspired by the published collections of Scott (*Minstrelsy Of The Scottish Border*) and Jamieson (*Popular*

74

Ballads & Songs) both of which appeared between 1802 and 1806. The popular success of these two collections, and the Scottish primacy in popular balladry they reclaimed from Percy's, inspired a small clan to continue their work. Robert Scott was presumably one of this clan, albeit an unsung member.

The Glenbuchat ballad ms. does not simply provide another source for Scottish oral variants of the Child 'canon'. By Glenbuchat's geographic position, "on the hilly western borders of Aberdeenshire,"[7] and the time Scott's collection was made, between 1808 - when the reverend arrived in the parish - and 1818, according to a later hand on the contents page of the ms., it provides a second early nineteenth-century source for ballad texts from Northeast Scotland, a source independent of those utilized by Peter Buchan in similar environs over the ensuing decade. Indeed, two of Buchan's most castigated texts, 'Lady Isabel' ("Stanzas 20, 21 ... are a commonplace, and a foolish one"[8]) and 'The New Slain Knight' ("A large part of this piece is imitated or taken outright from very well known ballads"[9]), turn out to have lost brothers in Scott's ms. as does 'James Herries'. An eighteen-verse version of Child Ballad #243 is listed under the title 'Lady Jane'.

'Lady Jane', despite its share of idiosyncracies, clearly derives from the same strain as Buchan's 'James Herries'. Unfortunately, the Glenbuchat 'Lady Jane' comes from a dislocated tradition some generations removed from its source. Though verses 2,9 and 11 establish an important bridge between 'the Buchan strain' and texts collected further south by Scott and Motherwell, 'Lady Jane' is some way further from its original template than Buchan's 26 verses. Bertrand Bronson unwittingly described the symptons of 'Lady Jane's degeneration when writing generically about "the inaction of tradition":

> **If [the ballad] is flourishing in tradition, the individual's loss will be made good by other singers, and violent change will be corrected. But where, after the lapse of years or exposure to new and untraditional ways, a singer has to restore rather than recall, the probability of major alteration is obviously very great. This ... is not to be attributed to the action, but rather, to the inaction, of tradition.[10]**

'Lady Jane' suggests a song barely hanging by its iambic feet to the audible voice of British tradition. Sections of the song smack of acts of restoration from a faintly recalled outline. The first verse certainly suggests one commonplace has been inserted at the very outset, at the expense of both the familiar "well met, well met" *and* Buchan's 'revenant' opening. If my assumption holds, that Buchan's opening represents authentic tradition, then the Glenbuchat variant had already interacted with a second strain:

> 1. Good morrow, good morrow Lady Jane
> Good morrow unto thee
> I am come to claim my former vows
> The vows ye made to me.[11]

In the second verse Lady Jane kindly affirms an earlier supposition of mine, referring to "our [joint] vows" before disavowing them.

The lady's Christian name coincides with the Price broadside, presumably because the version Price knew identified the lady along with that of the returning sailor. Jane hardly qualifies as a common moniker in traditional balladry, being a somewhat Anglicized equivalent of Jeannie (Buchan's preferred choice). Indeed its appearance here appears to be unique. That the debt again devolves to Price is suggested by the complete absence of shared imagery though, like Buchan, Scott's text confirms verse 19 of the 'James Harris' broadside to be a corrupt form of some traditional original:

PRICE	GLENBUCHAT
And now I am returnd again,	O speak not of your former vows
To take thee to my wife,	For that would be but strife
And thou with me shalt go to sea,	Ye'll speak no more of our former vows
To end all further strife.[7]	For I'm become a wife.

If in 'Lady Jane' the implication is that he has returned to her as a result of the broken vow, and she must now honour her vow by going with him, it shares just one other motif with the broadside. Verse 25 in Price runs thus:

> I have seven ships upon the sea;

> When they are come to land,
> Both mariners and marchandize
> Shall be at thy command [12]

Buchan's text avoids a clumsy notion like "merchandise ... at thy command." His reciter preferred something coined from the traditional lexicon, something as ungrammatically evocative as "wealth in every hand":

> See ye not yon seven pretty ships?
> The eighth brought me to land,
> With merchandize and mariners,
> And wealth in every hand. [13]

The final line of verse six in Scott, "And mirth on ilka hand," lays less emphasis on riches but otherwise confirms the traditional pedigree of Buchan's text.

Indeed six of the next seven verses are parallelled in Buchan's text, though only on one occasion does Scott suggest a superior reading. Buchan takes two verses [eleven and twelve], and unnecessarily introduces a sleeping husband, to achieve the same as Scott's verse seven. 'Lady Jane' does not make the husband a carpenter, but "a gallant lord." It is impossible at this point to know definitively whether some singer 'gentrified' the humble ship-carpenter. However, it is unlikely that our lady would have been enticed by her former lover's ships if she was already married to a lord:

> 3. I'm married to a gallant lord   [Buchan 3]
> An a good husband is he
> O go an seek another love
> An think no more o me.

> 4. [I] might a married a king's daughter [Buchan 4]
> So far ayont the sea
> But I left behind the robes o gowd
> An cam for love an thee.

> 5. O what woud we hae to live on [Buchan 8]

Tho I woud wi you gang
O I hae seven bonny ships
An the eight brought me to lan.

6. O I hae seven bonny ships [Buchan 9]
An the eight brought me to lan
Of merchandise and mariners
And mirth on ilka han.

7. She took up her bonny young son [Buchan 11+12]
An gae him a single kiss
I wadna for a thousand crowns
My good lord kent o this.

8. She lookit again to her bonny young son
The tear maist blint her ee
Dear hae I lovd an dearly agen
Ere I'd leave thy father an thee.

9. The robes that lady put on [Buchan 13]
Were gallant to behold
The belt that was roun her fair middle jimp
Was o the beaten gold.

The next verse does not find a parallel in Buchan, though it does share a similar opening line ("She turned her round upon the shore..." in Buchan), suggesting a common source. Neither remarks upon the mariners, as other texts do. The Glenbuchat ms. fails to comment on the ship's splendour, as other sources suggest it should:

10. As she gaed down to yon shore side
An down by yon sea strand
She set her foot on good ship board
An nimbly took the faem.

The eleventh verse almost exactly duplicates a verse absent from Buchan but collected by Scott and Motherwell in the lowlands. It also tallies with the Greig fragment - collected in the North East a hundred years hence - though Greig's singer's failed to align the storm with "her love's countenance":

> 11. She hadna been upon the sea
> A day but barely three
> Till changd grew her love's countenance
> An stormy grew the sea.

'Lady Jane' returns to the Buchan strain with verse thirteen, featuring that all-important reference to the banks, nay braes, of Italy. This time they are not littered with white lillies but with a rather more enticing prospect, red gold growing wild:

> 12. O if I were at hame again [Buchan 15]
> My good husband wi me
> There's no a man upon the earth
> Should see my face at sea.

> 13. O what ails thee dear love he said [Buchan 16]
> To look so sour on me
> I'll shew you how the red gowd grows
> O the braes of Italy.

At this point Scott and Buchan temporarily part company again. Verses fourteen to sixteen of Scott smack of 'violent change' by one hand. Verses 14 and 16 find no parallels in extant tradition, clumsily reiterating the homesick sentiments of verse 12 while, the menace implicit in verse eleven has been allowed to remain undeveloped. Evidently the interpolator's additions only ever had a localised popularity as they do not crop up in any of the other texts collected in Scotland in the first three decades of the nineteenth century.

Verse 15 seeks to suggest a promise of better days ahead, when all Lady Jane will drink shall be sweet, white, Spanish wine (?). It sits ill with the previous change in her lover's countenance and the even starker transformation three verses hence. If this were a Buchan text, Child would doubtless have vented his literary spleen on such obviously interpolated verses, suggesting a song isolated from root tradition for a generation or more:

14. But o if I were at hame again
My young son on my knee
There is no man upon the earth
Should gar me take the sea.

15. O what ails you my love he said
To sit so sad in min
Ye never shall drink the wan water
But the good Malaga wine.

16. But o if I were at hame again
My young son on my knee
And my good husband me beside
I never shoud take the sea.

The Glenbuchat ms. reverts to something like the Buchan strain for its denouement, as well as tallying well with Gavin Greig. As with Greig, there is no 'moralizing coda', suggesting that Buchan's strain probably once ended with the dramatic sinking of the ship by the lover's hand and that Buchan's coda was an interpolation by someone struck down by 'the broadside effect'. The penultimate verse of Scott preserves the all-important 'narrative repetition':

17. If ye winna be pleased wi the red gowd grown [Buc21]
On the braes o Italy
I'll shew you how the white fish swims
In the bottom o the sea.

18. Then he stood up a black black man
The ship nae miths did [keep]
He gart her gae wethershins [about]
An sunk her in the deep.

This final verse requires its own set of notes and queries. The imagery is very different from Greig and Buchan. Indeed it finds no correspondent in the 'Dæmon Lover' canon. But the "black, black man" is a glorious image, suggesting both the diabolic and the angry. Though in context he appears to be curiously mortal, driven to punish Lady Jane more for her ingratitude than her broken vow, the unnamed lover again sinks the ship

80

in a fury, the question of whether this is an act of supernatural vengeance having been rendered ambiguous by the imagery employed in the final couplet. In fact, the interpolator - for one was surely at work here - has surely taken his or her imagery from a familiar source, the beautiful 'Lowlands of Holland', in which:

> But the weary wind began to rise,
> And the sea began to rout,
> My love then and his bonny ship
> Turned withershins about.[14]

The final verse of 'Lady Jane' suggests a reworking by someone who recalled aspects of its conclusion - the diabolic countenance of the lover, sinking the ship by his own hand - and, lacking a keen balladic imagination, took from one who had. The picture of the 'revenant' as a "black, black man" provides a quite different image to that of the Buchan variant, though it does sit comfortably with that change in countenance in verse 11, a verse absent from Buchan. This charred image appears to suggest, albeit obliquely, an altogether different identity for our returned lover, one that ties the Glenbuchat text to a quite separate Scottish tradition - one that made the former lover not a revenant but the Devil himself; delayed the revelation of his identity to song end; and incorporated an apocalyptic dialogue between the Devil and the lady, taken from a fourteenth century romance concerning the adventures of one of Scotland's most mythic figures. Hence 'The Dæmon Lover'.

(vii) Scott of Abbotsford.

**[My singer] likewise sung part of a very beautiful ballad
which I think you will not have seen. As a punishment for
her inconstancy, the Devil is supposed to come and entice
a young woman from her husband, in the form of her
former lover. The tune is very solemn and melancholy,
and the effect is mixed with a considerable proportion of
horror. - William Laidlaw.[1]**

Establishing the revenant nature of the former lover adds an important
dimension to an otherwise mundane tale of temptation and guilt. What it
does not afford is an explanation of the supernatural powers with which
our 'Dæmon Lover' is endowed on his return. The final verse of the
Greig-Buchan text confirms that it is the spirit of 'James Harris' that
causes the ship to sink (unlike in the familiar broadside texts); that the
storm is invoked by the revenant; and that the white lillies on the banks
of Italy were intended to contrast with the white fishes/lillies at the bottom
of the sea. Though Buchan's text does not depict the advent of the
storm, Robert Scott's North Eastern text does, as do both of William
Motherwell's variants, his *Minstrelsy* text bearing the more authentic
tone:

> They had not sailed a mile awa,
> Never a mile but three,
> When dark, dark, grew his eerie looks,
> And raging grew the sea.[2]

Motherwell's nine-verse text appeared in the 1827 edition of his
Minstrelsy, Ancient & Modern. An American text, collected from New
England by the same indefatigible collector who had previously located
the 'George Allis' fragment, suggests that Motherwell's text drew upon
an enduring tradition. This eight-verse 'condensation', transcribed in
October 1945, despite narrative holes, is an excellent text, another rare
rendition to have survived in America without the debilitating input of De
Marsan. It also adds an important piece to our jigsaw - the notion of the
lady in the song becoming increasingly aware that her former lover is
not all that he seems. In the Motherwell-Price text/s encroaching dread

consumes the song long before the destruction of the ship.

Thankfully not only did one Edith Ballenger Price, from Newport, Rhode Island, recall that fine verse about "his eerie looks" but she also provided the only American text to date to contain an all-important reference to "his cloven foot." The image of the lady catching sight of 'her lover's' cloven foot is one of the most dramatic snapshots in all of popular balladry. Ms. Price says that she learnt the song from a lady whose family came from England, the only real suggestion that the 'dæmonic' version might have once had a foothold in English tradition. Comparing Ms. Price's rendition with the one in Motherwell's *Minstrelsy* affords an invaluable insight into how the strings of tradition can preserve the supernatural. The similarities are striking:

MOTHERWELL	PRICE
1. I have seven ships upon the sea, Laden with the finest gold, And mariners to wait us upon; All these you may behold.	1. I've seven ships upon the sea, Beaten w/ the finest gold, And mariners to wait upon us; All this she shall behold.
2. And I have shoes for my love's feet, Beaten of the purest gold, And lined wi' the velvet soft, To keep my love's feet from the cold.	2. She set her foot unto the ship No mariners did she behold, But the sail was o' the [finest silk] And the mast o' the beaten gold.
3. O how do you love the ship? he said. Or how do you love the sea? And how do you love the bold mariners That wait upon thee and me?	
4. O I do love the ship, she said, And I do love the sea; But woe be to the dim mariners, That nowhere I can see!	
5. They had not sailed a mile awa, Never a mile but one, When she began to weep and mourn,	3. They hadna' sailed a league, a league, A league but only one, When she began to weep & to mourn,

83

And to think on her wee little son.	And to think on her little wee son.

6. O hold your tongue, my dear, he said,
And let all your weeping abee,
For I'll soon show to you how the lilies grow,
On the banks of Italy.

4. Now hold ye tears, my dearest dear;
Let all your weeping be;
For I'll show you how the lilies grow,
On the banks of Italy.

7. They had not sailed a mile awa,
Never a mile but two,
Until she espied his cloven foot,
From his gay robes sticking thro.

5. They hadna' been a league, a league,
A league but only two,
When she beheld his cloven foot,
From his gay robe thrusting through.

8. They had not sailed a mile awa,
Never a mile but three,
When dark, dark, grew his eerie looks
And raging grew the sea.

6. They hadna' sailed a league, a league,
A league but only three,
When dark & fearsome grow his looks
And gurly grow the sea.

7. Now hold your tears, my dearest dear,
Let all your weeping be
& I'll show ye how the white lilies grow
At the bottom o' the sea.

9. They had not sailed a mile awa
Never a mile but four,
When the little wee ship ran round about,
And never was seen more.[3]

8. They hadna' sailed a league, a league,
A league but only four;
When the little wee ship ran round about
And never was seen more.[4]

Perhaps one is doing Ms. Price a disservice referring to her rendition as a condensation. Her eight verses accord remarkably well with Motherwell's nine. Perhaps, as the English and American broadsides elected to start the tale in act three, some long-forgotten Scottish wag decided to take Mr. Graves at his word and begin proceedings in "the last act of the play." As it is, Motherwell's reciter and Ms. Price both start and end on the same verse and inbetween agree on all the main particulars (the absence of mariners, the banks of Italy, the cloven foot, the raging sea and a fine 'lingering' quartet that builds to its climax four miles/leagues from shore).

Indeed, the two texts - recorded a hundred and twenty five years and three thousand miles apart - correspond so well that it begs the question: could Motherwell's version, which was after all a published text, have spawned its own rivulet of tradition? I think not. Setting aside the fact that Motherwell's work remained largely unknown outside antiquarian circles (and indeed the text in question Motherwell only apologetically included as a preface for what he deemed the more authoritative version, t'wit that published by Scott), the imagery in Price's rendition is, if anything, *more* convincing than Motherwell's. In particular, the penultimate verse, slightly Anglicized in Motherwell, rings with an authentic Scottish brogue in Price:

> They hadna' sailed a league, a league,
> A league but only three,
> When dark and fearsome grow his looks
> And gurly grow the sea.[5]

I presume that our New England lady was not in the habit of using the word 'gurly' despite the fact that, when imbued with some vocal gravel, it acquires a fine onomatopoeic quality. That her recollection had an authentic basis can be confirmed by reference to page 297 of George Kinloch's manuscript:

> Till grim, grim grew his countenance,
> And gurly grew the sea.[6]

Ms. Price's version also bypasses the strange offer made by the revenant, "mariners to wait upon us" - subsequently contradicted by the lady's protestation, "woe be to the dim mariners/ that nowhere can I see!" In Ms. Price's rendition, "She set her foot unto the ship/ no mariners did she behold." Her second verse, though it finds no real parallel in Motherwell, replicates - almost word-for-word - verse nine of Scott. The absence of mariners on this spectral ship is a lovely touch, one whose disappearance (sic) from tradition is much to be mourned.

Walter Scott's source, Walter Grieve, concentrated wholly on the revenant's demeanour, not offset by any concomitant drama on the seas:

> She had not sailed a league, a league,

85

A league but barely three,
When dismal grew his countenance,
And drumlie grew his e'e.[7]

However, Walter Grieve may simply have recalled the final line incorrectly (e'e, i.e. eye, for sea). The Glenbuchat version has the same verse - even down to the use of "countenance" - but the final line reads, "An stormy grew the sea." The storm-as-portent should surely be the preferred text, contributing as it does to a sense of impending doom - even if Scott's text has enjoyed posterity's favour at the expense of all others.

Scott's abiding interest in ballads was first instilled by his juvenile acquisition of Bishop Percy's hugely successful if provocative *Reliques of Ancient English Poetry*, published in 1765 and enough of a culture-shock to inspire almost universal endorsement from London's notoriously divisive literary circles. Scott later confessed, "I do [not] believe I ever read a book half so frequently, or with half the enthusiasm."[8] The first edition of Scott's *Minstrelsy Of The Scottish Border*, published between 1802 and 1803, came about as a result of his desire to do the same for Scotland.

Despite his title, Percy had included a substantial wedge of the best Scottish ballads - the likes of 'Sir Patrick Spens', 'Edward' and 'Lord Thomas and Fair Annie'. He also carried on correspondence with literate Scots regarding other treasures as yet unexcavated (some of his papers were eventually made available, along with his fabled folio, in the mid-nineteenth century, affording Child previously unpublished variants from the Percy archive).

Scott, who felt aggrieved at some of Percy's assumptions, set out to produce a wholly Scottish collection of ballads. In this he was not alone. Both David Herd and Joseph Ritson had published collections of Scottish songs in the last quarter of the eighteenth century. As with his English collections, Ritson's was entirely drawn from written sources but Herd's came from recitation, making him the first antiquarian to actually tap directly into oral tradition.

Scott, enlisting various helpers, sought to combine both approaches, drawing on singers and manuscripts. Having accessed the papers of Burns' friend, Robert Riddell, and Mrs. Brown of Falkland, he enlisted others to scout for oral sources. Scott's most productive helper 'in the field' was one William Laidlaw. It was Laidlaw who, in a letter to Scott, dated January 3, 1803, recounted his first encounter with the old man, Walter Grieve, and gave a half-remembered outline of a ballad Grieve had sung for him:

I remember but very few verses. He prevails upon her to go [aboard] to hear his musicians after upbraiding her,
> I might hae marrit a king's daughter,
> but I mindit my love for thee.

The description of her setting her child on the nurse's knee and bidding him farewell is waesome, but I have forgot it.

> She set her foot into the ship,
> To hear the music play;
> The masts war o the beaten goud,
> And the sails o the silk sae gay.

> They hadna saild a league thrae land,
> A league but barely three,
> Till drearie grew his countenance,
> And drumlie grew hie ee.

> They hadna saild another league,
> Another league but three,
> Till she beheld his cloven fit,
> And she wept most bitterlie.

> 'O had yer tongue, my love,' he said,
> 'Why weep ye sae mounfulie?
> We're gaun to see how the lillies do grow
> On the banks o fair Italie.'

> 'What hills are yon, yon pleasant hills,
> Where the sun shines...?'
> 'O yon's the hills of heaven,' he said,
> 'Where you will never win!'.[9]

Though Laidlaw evidently returned to collect a full text, it would not be included in Scott's *Minstrelsy* until its fifth edition, some nine years later. In his letter - quoted at the beginning of the chapter - Laidlaw implies that the singer was in no doubt as to the true identity of the 'dæmon lover' - the Devil - nor his motive for his curious mission - "to punish her for her inconstancy."

The *Minstrelsy* - which also carried a preface on the nature of popular poetry and long, speculative introductions, like the 78-page essay 'On the Fairies of Popular Superstition' that precedes 'Tam Lin' - was the most successful work of its kind since *Reliques*. However, it was also apparent from the outset that Scott had no more presented the authentic texts of Scottish singers than Percy had resisted meddling with his originals. In at least two instances, a turgid epic called 'Auld Maitland' and the livelier 'Kinmont Willie', Scott has long been suspected of 'reconstructing' the ballads not from tradition, but from his own imagination (Scott, somewhat disingenuously, admits in his introduction to 'Kinmont Willie' that "the ballad is preserved by tradition ... but much mangled by reciters; so that some conjectural emendations have been absolutely necessary"[10]). Child could not resist including 'Kinmont Willie' in *English And Scottish Popular Ballads*, even though the song has never been recovered by any other Scottish collector.

Scott later professed to recant his original methodology, founded on the belief that one could somehow weld the best versions from tradition into one cogent whole. In an extraordinary letter to William Motherwell in 1825, he sought to convince Motherwell not to travel the same path, but to faithfully set down what he had collected "from the mouths of the people":

> **I think I did wrong myself in endeavouring to make the best possible set of an ancient ballad out of several copies obtained from different quarters, and that, in many respects, if I improved the poetry, I spoiled the simplicity of the old song. There is no wonder this should be the case when one considers that the singers or reciters by whom the ballads were preserved and handed down, must, in general, have had a facility, from memory at least, if not from genius (which they might often possess), of filling up verses which they had forgotten, or altering such as they might think they could improve. Passing through this process in different parts of**

the country, the ballads, admitting that they had one common poetical
original (which is not to be inferred merely from the similitude of the
story), became, in progress of time, totally different productions, so far as
the tone and spirit of each is concerned. In such cases, perhaps, it is as well
to keep them separate, as giving in their original state a more accurate idea
of our ancient poetry, which is the point most important in such
collections.[11]

Despite voicing such commendable sentiments, Scott never did much to
correct his own work. However, he did leave behind him a collection of
Materials for the Border Minstrelsy which Child was belatedly able to
access (Child's amendations appeared in 1892 in the 'Additions &
Corrections' section of the fourth volume to ESPB). Unfortunately, the
version of 'The Dæmon Lover' that first appeared in the fifth edition of
the *Minstrelsy* in 1812 does not appear in its virgin state among the
Abbotsford materials. As such, reconstructing something approximating
to a 'traditional Scott version' may require a little circumnavigation of its
own.

Motherwell, when he wrote to Scott, was far advanced with his own
Minstresly, Ancient & Modern, and though he did take Scott's advice on
board he probably always intended to reproduce the ballads "in their
original state [as] a more accurate idea of our ancient poetry." His view
of Scott's work may have been laudatory, but this did not stop him
casting aspersions in his *Minstrelsy* in the direction of Scott's
correspondent, William Laidlaw, the man who provided Scott with what
purported to be Walter Grieve's rendition of 'The Dæmon Lover', of
which Motherwell wrote:

> It would be unfair to imagine for a moment that the Editor of the
> meritorious work now quoted made any addition to this ballad, other than
> was furnished by his correspondent; but, Mr. Laidlaw, it is suspected, may
> have improved [sic] upon its naked original ... [My G text] is but a meagre
> skeleton of Mr. Laidlaw's edition, which it will be observed is embellished
> with diverse "pleasant hills and dreary mountains of snow," not to be
> found in any charts of those days ... Another circumstance in which they
> vary, is in the remarkable progressive growth of the Dæmon Lover as they
> near the "dreary mountains."[12]

And yet, contained within Motherwell's ms. is a second text [Child's E text] self-evidently 'acquired' after these comments were written. There are large sections that accord with the Laidlaw-Scott text, particularly those final verses, as a comparison may perchance illustrate:

SCOTT	MOTHERWELL ['E']
1.O where have you been, my long, long lover This long seven years and mair? O I'm come to seek my former vows Ye granted me before.	Where have you been, my long lost love This seven long years and more? I've been seeking gold for thee, my love And riches of great store.
	2.Now I'm come for the vows you promised You promised me long ago; ...
2. O hold your tongue of your former vows, For they will breed sad strife, O hold your tongue of your former vows, For I am become a wife	.... My former vows you must forgive, For I'm a wedded wife
3. He turned him right and round about, And the tear blinded his e'e; I wad never ha'e trodden on Irish ground, If it had not been for thee.	
4. I might ha'e had a king's daughter, Far, far beyond the sea; I might have had a king's daughter, Had it not been for love o' thee.	3. I might have been married to a king's dau Far, far ayont the sea; But I refused the crown of gold, And it's all for the love of thee.
5. If ye might have had a king's daughter, Yer sel ye had to blame; Ye might have taken the king's daughter, For ye kend that I was nane.	4. If ye might have married a king's daughte Yourself you have to blame;....
	.... For I'm married to a ship's-carpenter And to him I have a son.
6. If I was to leave my husband dear, And my two babes also, O what have you to take me to,	5. Have you any place to put me in,

90

Dylan's Daemon Lover

If with you I should go?

7. I ha'e seven ships upon the sea -
Th eighth brought me to land -
With four-and-twenty bold mariners,
And music on every hand.

8. She has taken up her two little babes
Kissd them baith cheek and chin;
'O fair ye weel, my ain two babes
For I'll never see you again.

9. She set her foot upon the ship,
No mariners could she behold;
But the sails were o' the taffetie,
And the masts o' the beaten gold.

10. She had not sailed a league, a league
A league but barely three,
When dismal grew his countenance,
And drumlie grew his e'e.

If I with you should gang?
I've seven brave ships upon the sea,
All laden to the brim.

6. I'll build my love a bridge of steel,
All for to help her o'er;
Likewise webs of silk down by her side,
To keep my love from the cold.

7.She took her eldest son into her arms,
And sweetly did him kiss:
My blessings go with you, & your father too
For little does he know of this.

8. As they were walking up the street,
Most beautiful for to behold,
He cast a glamour o'er her face,
And it shone like the brightest gold.

9. As they were walking along the seaside,
Where his gallant ship lay in,
So ready was the chair of gold
To welcome this lady in.

10. They had not sailed a league, a .league
A league but scarcely three,
Till altered grew his countenance,
And raging grew the sea.

11. They had not sailed a league, a league
A league but barely three,
Until she espied his cloven foot,
And she wept right bitterlie.

12. O hold your tongue of your weeping, says he,
Of your weeping now let me be;
I will shew you how the lilies grow
On the banks of Italy.

11. When they came to yon seaside,
She set her down to rest,
It's then she spied his cloven foot,
Most bitterly she wept.

12. O is it for gold that you do weep?
Or is it for fear?
Or is it for the man you left behind
When that you did come here?

13. It is not for gold that I do weep,
O no, nor yet for fear,
But it is for the man I left behind
When that I did come here.

13. O what hills are yon pleasant hills,
That the sun shines sweetly on?
O yon are the hills of heaven, he said,
Where you will never win.

14. O whaten a mountain is yon, she said,
All so dreary wi' frost and snow?
O yon is the mountain of hell, he cried,
Where you and I will go.

14. O what a bright, bright hill is yon,
That shines so clear to see
O it is the hill of heaven, he said,
Where you shall never be.

15. O what a black, dark hill is yon,
That looks so dark to me?
O it is the hill of hell, he said,
Where you and I shall be.

16. Would you wish to see the fishes swim
In the bottom of the sea,
Or wish to see the leaves grow green
On the banks of Italy.

17. I hope I'll never see the fishes swim
On the bottom of the sea,

But I hope to see the leaves grow green
On the banks of Italy.

15. He strack the tap-mast wi' his hand,
The fore-mast wi' his knee,
And he brake the gallant ship in twain,
And sank her in the sea.[13]

18. He took her up to the topmast high,
To see what she could see,
He sunk the ship in a flash of fire,
To the bottom of the sea.[14]

Scott's final verse is justifiably famous, but it is shot through with a certain self-consciousness hardly typical of the traditional ballad. Laidlaw later owned up to adding some four verses (6, 12, 17 and 18 in the 1812 edition) in correspondence with Scott, "to complete the fragment." These do not feature as part of Motherwell's E text and subsequent collections have tended to omit them (as I have). However, the final verses cannot be dismissed as wholly Scott's (or Laidlaw's) since Buchan's, Greig's, Robert Scott's and Motherwell's 'E' text all bring the ballad to a supernatural climax.

Motherwell's latterday text, of unknown provenance, comes very close to Scott's in that final verse. Though it also includes her espying his cloven foot this comes, somewhat incongruously, "when they came to yon seaside," so that one suspects the conflation of two verses - Scott 11 and Glenbuchat 10. It also includes those 'hills of heaven and hell', which do not feature in Buchan, and which Motherwell had previously cast doubt upon. Evidently he came upon a rendition that required a rethink.

The 1803 letter, both of Motherwell's texts and the version collected in Vermont from Ms. Price all affirm Scott's dæmonic revenant as drawn from authentic tradition. Yet Scott and Motherwell [E] remain the only British traditional texts to feature the 'heaven and hell' verses. The earliest texts (both broadsides) and the most 'complete' traditional version (Buchan's) omit said verses; and Motherwell not only had yet to encounter these verses when compiling his *Minstrelsy*, but queried their authenticity. It seems unlikely that Motherwell's insinuations regarding external input would have prompted either Scott or Laidlaw to provide their text as collected as a rebuttal to his accusations.

Motherwell's E text itself contains some curious elements. Its tendency

93

to veer into an almost Anglicized paraphrase of traditional verse ("I'm come for the vows") strongly suggests that, rather than being written down directly from "the mouths of the people," it is a half-remembered recollection of an oral rendition (or two). The crucial "broken vows" verse in Scott, also found in American tradition, only appears in Motherwell as a paraphrased substitute of its traditional self. Verse nine of Scott - replicated in Ms. Price's eight-verse 'condensation' - is entirely omitted and, though the 'banks of Italy' occupy two verses [16-17] they have lost the impact of their once-characteristic 'narrative repetition'. Verses three, nine and twelve in Scott are not replicated in Motherwell but - save for the surely Jacobite interpolation, "I wad never ha'e trodden on Irish ground" - find traditional corollaries that lend them credence.

On the other hand, of the seven verses in Motherwell without parallel in Scott, verses six and nine smack of the commonplace, are not found elsewhere in the 'House Carpenter' family (unless verse nine is a distant relative of Glenbuchat 10), and cry of interpolations that quickly passed from favour. Verses twelve/thirteen, and sixteen/seventeen duplicate familiar dialogue in an unfamiliar way - the lillies of Italy have become "leaves grow green," clearly some combination of mishearing, misunderstanding and/or misapplication of the former image. 'Fear' as a mistranscription of 'fee' also rears up again in verses twelve and thirteen.

Verses that almost replicate themselves but advance the tale subtly remain perhaps the most common of ballad conventions - the phrase 'incremental repetition' was coined to express the technique - but here the dialogue does not function in a 'balladic' way, failing to bring the imminence of her doom home to the lady. What we have instead is mere reiteration. Verses 12-13 and 16-17 certainly have a basis in tradition but they have been badly mangled. However, not all of the verses unique to Motherwell's 'E' text come across as suspect. Verse eight is something else altogether, a verse which has coursed through tradition, even when diluted by the forces of rationalization and sentimentalization (it is discussed at length in the next chapter).

Unfortunately, we do not know where Motherwell got his 'E' text. Though he usually cited his sources in his manuscript, in the case of 'The Dæmon Lover' he did not. Nor do the manuscript and his *Minstrelsy* tally as much as one might expect. As Mary Ellen Brown recently wrote, "the

Manuscript was a carefully copied record of the ballads Motherwell *and others* [my italics] collected after the *Minstrelsy* was already in process."[15] It is a tad strange that the ballad should appear so early in the manuscript (pp97 of the 677-page ms.) if Motherwell came upon this text after the *Minstrelsy* was completed. There is certainly no mention of the song being collected from the "Old Singing Women" of Renfrewshire in Motherwell's ballad notebook, now housed at Harvard.

Discounting the interpolated verses that are mere embroidery, duplicated dialogue and paraphraseology, Motherwell's E text accords well with Scott's, surely a corrupted example of the same strain. They both recognize the importance of the 'broken vows'; they both refer to the king's daughter he forsook; they each note the raging sea; they share the cloven foot; they both have banks of Italy, hills of heaven and hell and the destruction of the ship by supernatural means at the hand of the former lover. It is no great stretch to view Scott's published version as a reworked proximate of Motherwell E. Though considerably less corrupt than our 'E' text, Scott's may itself have suffered the loss of a couple of verses - a second 'banks of Italy' and Motherwell's verse eight - in its passage through the centuries.

If Scott's and Motherwell's texts do reflect the same strain, we are left with a solitary example of a (quite possibly localized) text. This need not preclude the possibility that said text reflects the original 'Dæmon Lover' template better than any other Scottish text. It simply suggests a single point of tradition for a particular, highly dramatic, conclusion to 'The Dæmon Lover', one that makes its diabolic elements - exemplified by a cloven foot and the hills of heaven and hell - as central to our tale as the 'broken vows'.

(viii) Vulgar Rationalism.

> **In [the Price broadside, James Harris] expressly says to the woman, I brought you away to punish you for breaking your vows to me. This explicitness may be prosaic, but it seems to me regrettable that the conception was not maintained. To explain the eery personality and proceedings of the ship-master, [Motherwell and Scott,] with a sort of vulgar rationalism, turn him into the devil. - Professor Child.[1]**

As it happens, these dæmonic elements have powerful antecedents that take us deep into the netherworld of tradition, to the fifteenth century and the very dawn of traditional ballad forms. Child bemoans the appearance of the devil in the Scott and Motherwell texts but it is hard to see how the metamorphosis of a ghost returned from hell (and clearly this is from whence he came) into even the devil himself (a marginal adjustment) is an act of "vulgar rationalism," interpolated at a later date or not.

But then Child had a blind-spot on such matters ("Christianity and foreign culture ... have been equally destructive in their effects upon ancient national poetry"[2]). He remained uncomfortable with the notion that pagan superstition and devout Christianity had comfortably coexisted for centuries before the Reformation. In surmising that the diabolical nature of the revenant in 'The Dæmon Lover' was an exercise in 'vulgar rationalism' he was as wrong as when he asserted that "an 'unco[uth] knight', who is the devil," was "a departure from the proper story,"[3] in the very first entry in *English & Scottish Popular Ballads*, 'A Riddle Wisely Expounded'. The conclusion of Motherwell's text for Child Ballad No.1, much like his 'Dæmon Lover', reserves the revelation of an infernal origin to its "unco knight" until the final verse:

> As soon as she the fiend did name,
> He flew awa in a blazing flame.[4]

Child felt this reminded him "of the behavior of trolls and nixes under like circumstances."[5] Once again he preferred to make his 'A' text a

seventeenth century English broadside with a sentimental ending
grafted onto a traditional original:

> When she these questions answered had,
> The knight became exceeding glad.
>
> And having [truly] try'd her wit,
> He much commended her for it.
>
> And after, as it is verifi'd,
> He made of her his lovely bride.[6]

This time, though, Child was required to do a *volte face*. As an addition to
the very last volume of his *magnum opus*, he included a work entitled
'inter diabolus et virgo', from a ms. dated c.1445, the earliest ballad
template that can be directly connected to a proven - and, as of the
early twentieth century, extant - tradition (his one earlier text, 'Judas',
cannot be considered a ballad save by the most elastic criteria). Here,
self-evidently, was the 'original' strain from which 'Riddles Wisely
Expounded' ultimately sprung. A classic example of a fifteenth century
'battle of wits', 'Inter diabolus et virgo' revolves around the devil's
attempts to catch out a virgin. It ends, yet again, with his defeat:

> Now, thu fende, styl thu be;   *Now, oh fiend, be still,*
> Nelle ich speke no more with the![7]   *I'll speak no more with thee.*

Thus can the devil's appearance in popular balladry be shown to extend
back to the early fifteenth century, to the very birth of the ballad form.
The fiend in 'Riddles Wisely Expounded' became many things before it
was interred in print, a "fause knight," an "elfin knight" or simply a suitor,
but he was originally as diabolic in intent as our very own dæmon lover.
However, Motherwell's early nineteenth century text preserved his 'true'
nature; as, indeed, even more remarkably, did a solitary American
rendition collected by Miss Alfreda Peel in Virginia in 1922, and another
collected at around the same time in the counties of southern England
by the eccentric field-collector Alfred Williams:

> Then he clapped his wings, and aloud did cry
> And [in] a flame of fire he flew away.[8]

So an English manuscript of the mid-fifteenth century appears to document an early version of an authentic popular ballad that reappeared in Scottish tradition in the nineteenth century, and then in southern England and Virginia in the early twentieth century, dæmonic ending intact. Clearly, here was a ballad that, whatever its origins (and one suspects that, this time, they were English), became dispersed widely enough to remain in popular tradition until the early twentieth century, retaining, albeit tenuously, vestiges of its original template, affected - as it was bound to be - by more popular variants of its blackletter stepbrother.

In fact, 'vulgar rationalism' stripped the revenant in 'The Dæmon Lover' of his diabolic countenance, eventually making him no revenant at all. Since the only two Scottish texts to contain a vision of the hills of heaven and hell also make reference to the 'cloven foot', it seems logical to suppose that the cloven-footed revenant and 'the hills of heaven and hell' originally comprised parts of the same template. As it happens, despite the fact that they twice appear in tandem in Scottish oral tradition, the 'hills of heaven and hell' have been collected from American tradition at least thirty-two times and not once has the cloven foot accompanied them.

The sudden spying of the 'cloven foot', powerful an image as it is, has long struck me as a probable interpolation. Given its appearance in three early nineteenth century Scottish texts - representing two separate strains - the interpolation must have been adopted on a popular level for at least two or three generations, entering tradition no later than the late seventeenth century.

The incrementally repeating verses incorporating this graphic image suggest an interpolator conversant with balladic conventions and at ease with their appropriate usage. Verses of the version of 'Sir Patrick Spens' collected by Walter Scott that incrementally reveal the scale of a storm at sea do not juxtapose the macrocosmic (a violent storm at sea) with the personal (her imminent doom), as the 'interpolator' in 'The Dæmon Lover' has:

They hadna sailed a league, a league,   They had not sailed a mile awa,

A league but only three,
When the whirlin' wind an' the ugly jaws
Cam drivin to their knie.

Never a mile but two,
Until she espied his cloven foot,
From his gay robes sticking thro.

They hadna sailed a league, a league,
A league but only five,
When the whirlin' wind an' the ugly jaws
Their gude ship began to rive.

They had not sailed a mile awa,
Never a mile but three,
When dark, dark, grew his eerie looks,
And raging grew the sea.

They hadna sailed a league, a league,
A league but only nine,
When the whirlin' wind an' the ugly jaws
Cam drivin to their chin.[9]

They had not sailed a mile awa,
Never a mile but four,
When the little wee ship ran round about
And never was seen more.[10]

Fleming Andersen believes that these ballads share the same "presaging supra-narrative function," to quote a phrase. That is to say:

> The stanzas mark ominous transition towards disaster at sea ... heralding imminent danger for the person engaging in the formula's action. The formal structure underlines the stylistic effect, obviously working so well in an oral dramatic performance: the characters have not ... sailed far when...![11]

Though the convention in question ended up being utilized in such unregenerate twaddle as 'The George Aloe and the Sweepstake', it was also known to appear in some of the best sixteenth-century ballads ('The Golden Vanity', 'Henry Martyn'). In the diabolical template for 'The Dæmon Lover', there are precious few ballad commonplaces ("the dapple-grey steed," "the lily white hand," "the red rosy cheek" &c.). This in itself argues against eighteenth century composition, when such phrases had indeed become "the insignia of popular tradition," the advent of the broadside having begun to play its part in ossifying traditional imagery.

Presumably the aim of the interpolator (if that is what s/he was) was to add to the feeling of foreboding creeping o'er the song. Unfortunately it lessens the impact of the revelation, in the second 'hills of heaven and hell' exchange, that they are hellbound, and the revenant's assumption of supernatural proportions in that final verse.

It just so happens that the 'cloven foot' has a ballad antecedent all its own, located within the same family as the ballad just cited. Though 'The Devil's Courtship' was excluded from ESPB - its use of a burden not a refrain being deemed 'unballadic' by Child - it shares with Child Ballads 1, 'Riddles Wisely Expounded' and 3, 'The Fause Knight Upon the Road' a notion of the Devil come to tempt an innocent. However, the tempter in 'The Devil's Courtship' does not use riddles to confound a mortal, preferring the simpler expedient of bribing the unfortunate maiden into coming with him. The first ten verses in the best version known to Child simply raise the stakes from a "pennyworth of priens" to "a braw snuff box" to "a braw silk gown" to "a nine-stringed bell" to "a purse of gold," at which point our foolish maid finally agrees to ride off with the "kind Sir":

> Mount up Jack ye hae won the day,
> And wi' you I'll gang away.
>
> Burden: And I'll gang alang wi' you, my dear,
> And I'll gang alang wi' you.[12]

At this point the tenor of the tale dramatically shifts as the identity of the stranger is revealed to both maiden and audience (no balladic convention tips the listener off as to the stranger's true Self, unless one subscribes to the Gravesian theory that "a nine-stringed bell" would have been offered "because nine was the number sacred to the all-wise Moon-goddess Hecate"[13]). The change is reflected in a familiar sight and a new burden of regret, reiterated after the final verse:

> They had na gane a mile atweel
> Till she saw his fit cloven to the heel. [foot
>
> Burden: Sayand, I rue I cam wi' you, kind Sir,
> Sayand I rue I cam wi' you.
>
> I have gat you now I'll haud you fast,
> Gowd wan your virgin heart at last.
>
> Burden: An I'll no part wi' you, my dear,
> An I'll no part wi' you.

> Nae mair she said but went alang,
> At every mile that dulefu sang:

> Burden: I rue that I cam wi' you, kind Sir,
> I rue that I cam wi' you.[14]

This fine ballad - for, refrain or not, a ballad it surely is - was recorded by Andrew Crawfurd from a lady by the name of Mrs. Storie nee Mary MacQueen in December 1826. Though Crawfurd turned into quite a collector of ballads himself, at this stage he was engaged on William Motherwell's behalf, "aiding him with his Minstrelsy."[15] Indeed, fourteen items obtained from Mrs. Storie were included in Motherwell's own ms., thirteen of which were then utilized by Child in some form in ESPB. The exception was 'The Devil's Courtship', even though here was a ballad with a considerably greater pedigree than 'Fause Knight Upon the Road', Child's only complete text of which also came from Mrs. Storie.

Though it appears in none of the major nineteenth-century ballad collections, Child knew other variants of 'The Devil's Courtship'. He had access to Kinloch's manuscript, which contained a similar text collected in the 1820s. He also had occasion to call upon Robert Chambers' *Popular Rhymes of Scotland*, first published in 1826 and revised in 1841 and 1870, which itself contained a text of the ballad, entitled by Chambers 'The Tempted Lady'. Chambers' version prefers "seven silver hinges, and seven silver locks" to a "nine-stringed bell," and features a verse hinting of two paths, one righteous, one not:

> I'll gie you a pair o' bonny shoon,
> The tane made in Sodom, the tother in Rome.[16]

Sadly 'The Tempted Lady' ends in 'Riddle Wisely Expounded' fashion with the Devil flying off, this time with the "leddy" in tow, after she acccepts his final bribe, "the hale [whole] o' Bristol town." Though Chambers fails to give his source, he makes great play of the fact that his collection is compiled largely from oral sources. In the case of 'The Tempted Lady', the ballad has a long didactic introduction, presumably part of Chambers' original transcription, which provides us with a much-needed explanation of why that cloven foot has a tendency to make unwelcome appearances in such parables-in-song:

> **Noo, lasses, ye should never be owre proud; for ye see there was ance a leddy, and she was aye fond o' being brawer than other folk; so she gaed awa' to take a walk ae day, her and her brother: so she met wi' a gentleman - but it was nae gentleman in reality, but Auld Nick himsel', who can change himsel' brawly into a gentleman - a' but the cloven feet; but he keepit them out o' sight. So he began to make love to the young leddy....[17]**

'The Devil's Courtship' has been collected in both England and Scotland in the twentieth century, as 'The Keys of Canterbury' (not Bristol) in English tradition and as 'A Pennyworh o' Preens' in Scotland. Perhaps predictably, the twentieth century versions have dropped the dæmonic denouement, making the song a series of romantic enticements that finally convince our reluctant maiden to "gang alang." Even the "nine-stringed bell" has become merely "a braw silver bell."[18] Nevertheless, 'The Devil's Courtship' belongs to a once-vibrant genre: the diabolic ballad.

If the cloven-footed one walked all the way from 'The Devil's Courtship' to "take his bride away from the house carpenter," his absence from American tradition (Ms. Price excepted) suggests that the emigrants carrying the song overseas never knew this strain; or that it rapidly dropped from its transatlantic oral self; or, most likely, that the song was transmitted Stateside pre-interpolation.

The residues of a dæmonized 'original', still discernible in modern American tradition, suggest not only that 'the dæmon strain' must once have run both wide and deep, but that the strain was initially unfettered by cloven feet. Other clues affirm the dæmon strain as the original template. The moralizing coda found in Ms. Price and Motherwell's cloven-hoofed texts, though it may not have originated with the 'James Harris' broadside, remains the product of a sensibility affected by the broadside mindset - not that of a popular ballad *auteur* capable of appropriating visions of heaven and hell.

Cloven feet aside, the former lover's reappearance after seven years still ties him to the Devil's personal calendar of days, and whatever Child's convictions, no dæmonic guise in balladry ever suggested a latterday incursion into a non-dæmonized original. It is the modern variants of 'Riddles Wisely Expounded' and 'The Devil's Courtship' that have been exposed to the peddlers of "vulgar rationalism." 'The Dæmon Lover' meanwhile retains a sensibility all its own, a surreal twist in the tale making for a unique type of revenant ballad, suggesting a formative stage of development, unbound by conventionalities to come. What we have is a 'dæmon' ballad first and a 'ghost' ballad second, from a time when a "ghost is neither a pale wraith nor an emanation without substance."[19]

(ix) Passage to America.

Departure from their native country is no longer exile ... they carry with them their language, their opinions, their popular songs, and hereditary merriment: they change nothing but the place of their abode. - Samuel Johnson, 1773.[1]

Neither 'James Harris' nor 'The Distressed Ship Carpenter' have been collected in America in recognizable form, and yet some kind of rationalized English source certainly underlies Clay Walters' text, and must have impacted upon American tradition pre-De Marsan. At the same time, Scottish strains also left their imprint on American renditions. Having examined certain Scottish elements that barely survived the onset of the Industrial Revolution, we can now consider the Scottish motifs that crop up in American tradition, affirming that at some point a dual assault, English and Scottish, was made upon America by 'The Dæmon Lover'.

A key question is: when? According to David Hackett Fischer's epic history of the early British emigrations to North America, *Albion's Seed*, there were four primary waves of British emigration, spanning the years 1629 to 1775. If we discount the second wave of fleeing Royalists, the first and third waves were of a religious nature, reflecting a strain of the Protestant faith almost ascetic, and highly judgemental:

The first wave (1629-40) was an exodus of English Puritans who came mainly from the eastern counties and planted in Massachusetts a very special culture ... and a tradition of ordered liberty ... The third wave (ca. 1675-1715) ... carried yet another culture from the England's North Midlands to the Delaware Valley. It was founded on a Christian idea of spiritual equality, a work ethic of unusual intensity, a suspicion of social hierarchy, and an austerity which Max Weber called 'worldly asceticism'.[2]

Neither wave is very likely to have provided an appropriate conduit for supernatural strains of balladry. As the Annals of Philadelphia proclaimed, "We have not hoofs nor horns in our religion."[3] It is possible, though, that the *Diverting Songs* text of 'The Distressed Ship-Carpenter' may have crossed the water wide with the third wave from the North

Midlands (the song would be published in Newcastle as part of the *Rambler's Garland*).

If this was the case, this rationalized, moralizing variant was in competition with its northern parent-form from the very instance of its American assimilation. The original 'Dæmon Lover' strain would have been snapping at its heels. A series of first-class British ballad transmitters must have planted this tradition in American soil by the middle of the eighteenth century. This would have required something like the scale and geographic base/s of the fourth migration, which Fischer dates to the period 1717-1775:

> The magnitude of this movement was very large - more than a quarter-million people altogether. This was truly a mass migration, on a scale altogether different from the movements that had preceded it. Its rhythm was different too - not a single migration but a series of wavelike movements that continued through much of the eighteenth century. It also drew from a different part of Britain [to earlier emigrations]. Many of these people came from territories that bordered the Irish Sea - the north of Ireland, the lowlands of Scotland, and the northern counties of England ... This border region included six counties in the far north of England: Cumberland, Westmorland and parts of Lancashire on the western side of the Pennines; Northumberland, Durham and parts of Yorkshire to the east. It also embraced five counties of southern Scotland - Ayr, Dumfries, Wigtown, Roxburgh and Berwick. During the seventeenth century, its culture was carried westward across the Irish Sea to five counties of Ulster - Derry, Down, Armagh, Antrim and Tyrone.[4]

The borderers were migratory by nature, and the broad dissemination of Scottish ballads in America owes much to their willingness to endure hardships in the New World yet retain an emotional attachment to a core of Scottish lore. They were certainly plied with reasons to move on by the already settled British emigrants. The religious leaders had established their own stranglehold on the North Eastern seaboard, enclosing their urban enclaves in a moral code that held little appeal to borderers:

> With much encouragement from Quaker leaders, the North Britons moved rapidly westward from Philadelphia into the rolling hills of

the interior. **Many drifted south and west along the mountains of Maryland, Virginia and Carolinas.** *They gradually became the dominant English-speaking culture in a broad belt of territory that extended from the highlands of Appalachia through much of the Old Southwest.* **In the nineteenth century, they moved across the Mississippi River to Arkansas, Missouri, Oklahoma and Texas ... The distribution of surnames [in the 1790 census] shows that immigrants from North Britain found their way into every part of the American colonies but by far the largest concentration was to be found in the backcountry region that included southwestern Pennsylvania, the western parts of Maryland and Virginia, North and South Carolina, Georgia, Kentucky and Tennessee. Throughout that broad area, more than half of the population came from Scotland, Ireland and northern England.**[5]

These are precisely the districts where underlying strains of 'The Dæmon Lover' betray Scottish origins. The likelihood is that our ballad was carried from Scotland (and perhaps the borders of England) in the first drum-roll of this mass migration (i.e. @ 1717). Perhaps it had already passed to Ireland in the large-scale seventeenth-century migration of Scots to Ireland, being then carried 'across the pond' by Scots-Irish emigrants. Though 'The House Carpenter' has not been collected in Ireland, Irish balladry has perhaps delighted in the revenant form more than any other nation. The interaction between Scottish and Irish balladry would never again be as strong as in those years of migration.

What seems highly unlikely is that 'The Dæmon Lover' could have taken such a tenacious hold in America if it was reliant upon transmission from late eighteenth-century border emigrants. By the end of the century, as the *Rambler's Garland* reinforced a rationalized form for English readers, the Scottish strain was already lying down among the lowland heather.

One needs to recall just how much excavating of Scottish balladry was instigated by Percy's publication of *Reliques Of Ancient English Poetry*, gaining the (well-deserved) enmity of a generation of Scottish antiquarians for appropriating the best of Scottish ballads in the name of "the auld enemy." Over the next sixty years these antiquarians scoured the hills and valleys for the evidence to refute Percy's Anglocentric view of British balladry.

106

This unprecedented flood of Scottish ballad-collecting began with David Herd's 1769 volume, updated and expanded to two volumes by 1776. John Pinkerton (1783, 1786), Sir Walter Scott (1802-3), Robert Jamieson (1806), John Finlay (1808), Robert Hartley Cromek (1810), Alexander Laing (1822, 1823), Charles Kirkpatrick Sharpe (1823), James Maidment (1824, 1828), Peter Buchan (1825, 1828), Allan Cunningham (1825), Robert Chambers (1826, 1844), William Motherwell (1827) and George Kinloch (1827) all followed Herd's example, publishing their own collections of Scottish songmaking. Perhaps more important than any of these was the undertaking of Edinburgh publisher James Johnson, who endeavoured between 1787 and 1803 to publish a definitive collection of Scottish song in six volumes. Enlisting the ebullient Robert Burns in an editorial capacity just as the first volume of *The Scots Musical Museum* was going to press, Johnson discovered a willing conduit of both the traditional and the Burnsian, at least until Burns' tragically premature death, at the age of 33, in 1796.

Writers like Scott and Burns had access to manuscripts compiled by antiquarians like Robert Riddell of Glenriddell and James Skene of Rubislaw. Some contemporary mss., though, were not examined until Child undertook his great work. The so-called St. Clair manuscript, compiled in the 1770s, i.e. before any published collections save Percy and Herd, and Andrew Crawfurd's own manuscript, circa 1828, were largely unavailable to Child.

Yet none of these manuscripts contain a 'Dæmon Lover'. Nor did Herd encounter the song on his travels. If several antiquarians advanced on Herd's groundbreaking endeavours, 'The Dæmon Lover' eluded all save Buchan, Motherwell, Kinloch and the Scotts (admittedly the five most diligent Scottish collectors). Even Burns himself - who by his own admission first learnt ballads from a maid called Betty Davison who had "the largest collection in the county of tales and songs concerning ghosts, fairies, brownies, witches, apparitions, catraips, giants, inchanted towers, dragons and other trumpery"[6] - did not know the song, or at least did not recall it for Johnson's undertaking. It was even seemingly unknown to that great repository of ballads of superstition and romance, Mrs. Brown of Falkland.

And yet the wide dispersal of versions of 'The House Carpenter' in America presupposes a substantive popularity in oral tradition at the time of the major waves of emigration from the British mainland (it is unlikely that a 'House Carpenter' collected by Vance Randolph in the Ozarks comes from the same American original as a 'House Carpenter' collected by John Harrington Cox in West Virginia twenty years earlier - only a common British antecedent explains the scattered nature of Scottish motifs peeking through standardized American texts).

The notion that American strains of 'The Dæmon Lover' were transplanted during the early waves of emigration, i.e. no later than the mid-eighteenth century, finds a form of reverse corroboration in the almost total absence of renditions from the coastal outposts of Nova Scotia and Newfoundland. These two English colonies were inhabited by British settlers in the seventeenth and eighteenth centuries but in the case of Newfoundland the early settlers came almost exclusively from the Western counties of England - Hampshire, Dorset, Devon, Cornwall and Somerset - where the fishing trade had been a mainstay of the local economy for a thousand years. A list of settlers on the southern shore, compiled in 1675, contained only English names. The Irish began to settle there from 1713 on but Scots remained few and far between.

Nova Scotia, despite its name (New Scotland), bestowed on it in 1622 by Sir William Alexander, was not an inviting prospect for settlement until the French renounced all rights to the territory after the Seven Years War. As W.S. MacNutt observes, "The advance-guard of the great immigration of Highland Scots to Nova Scotia did not arrive until 1773, when *The Hector* came to Pictou via Philadelphia."[7] Not until the period 1801-1803, when eleven ships from Scotland arrived at Pictou, can "the great immigration" be said to have begun in earnest.

These two territories, early British settlements, as isolated by the sea as any Virginian mountain-range, might have been expected to yield a commensurate amount of British popular ballads. The yield has, if anything, been disproportionately small. Maud Karpeles, who visited Newfoundland in 1929, later wrote, "I had hoped that Newfoundland might yield a wealth of songs comparable with the riches that Cecil Sharp and I had discovered in the Southern Appalachian Mountains a decade earlier."[8] In fact, Karpeles found just 24 Child ballads - many badly mangled by tradition - in her excavations, compared with the 45 Child ballads Sharp and she had found in the hills of Eastern America. 'The Dæmon Lover', which had yielded 22 renditions in the Appalachians, failed to yield even a solitary fragment in Newfoundland. Kenneth Peacock's even more thorough excavations in the Fifties yielded but a single 'House Carpenter', and that an English broadside derivative. In Nova Scotia, neither Helen Creighton nor W. Roy MacKenzie succeeded in tracking down one 'Dæmon Lover'. Creighton's haul was a mere eleven Child ballads. MacKenzie reluctantly admitted, in his *The Quest Of The Ballad*, "I have not ceased to cherish the hope that I may yet extort from some crafty singer the admission that he knows 'a line or two' of 'James Harris' ... but so far I have had to content myself with the ... unsatisfying knowledge that [it was] ... once current in the northern part of Nova Scotia."[9]

That 'The Dæmon Lover' no longer enjoyed a motherland vogue by the end of the eighteenth century, when Herd and Burns were doing their excavations, and emigrants were abandoning Scotland for the promise of a New Scotland, seems confirmed by later Scottish collecting. Though Scotland did not benefit from the organized sweep undertaken by the English Folk Song Society in the first two decades of the twentieth century, four collectors covered the same territory as the likes of Buchan and Scott between 1904 and 1932, three with a methodical determination not known to any English collector, save Cecil Sharp himself. The collectors in question, Gavin Greig and J.B. Duncan, working in tandem, the American James Carpenter and, less significantly, John Ord, collected over a thousand Child variants between them. Yet Carpenter and Ord, collecting in the late twenties, never encountered 'The Dæmon Lover' even though Carpenter knew the song well, collecting two variants in North Carolina, whilst Greig and Duncan came up with a single five and a half verse fragment (see chapter four).

Evidently 'The Dæmon Lover' was at the height of its popularity in Britain in the late sixteenth and seventeenth century, the advent of the Age of Reason beginning its long, slow decline. In America it simultaneously embarked on an astonishing revival, but in a guise approximating to the 'rationalized' eighteenth-century English broadside. Curious.

It is unlikely that a song could reach America and thrive in the way 'The House Carpenter' must have *before* the mid-nineteenth century De Marsan broadside unless it was carried by several repositories of oral tradition. To find evidence of such pre-broadside transmission one needs to examine two specifically Scottish elements that, like that cloven foot, occasionally peak through a gay new guise.

The English tradition, far more convincingly assimilated by the De Marsan strain, had probably already 'evolved' into De Marsan's form by the time the latter was published. After all, though the act of publishing (and republishing) may be almost entirely responsible for 'The House Carpenter's perpetual reappearance in twentieth century America, De Marsan's text still clearly reflected an indigenous oral tradition.

Curiously, the broadside is missing one verse that remained part of the main template in American oral tradition well into the twentieth century. This verse contains one of three residual Scottish motifs unrepresented by 'James Harris', 'The Distressed Ship-Carpenter' or De Marsan. It was unquestionably part of transatlantic oral currency, along with "the banks of Italy" - less than a dozen examples - and the "hills of heaven and hell" - just over two dozen examples. The verse in question appears in nearly two-thirds of known American variants, usually in the form of:

> She dressed herself in rich attire,
> Most glorious to behold,
> And as she tread upon her road
> She shone like the glittering gold.[10]

The verse adds little to the story, does not fit with the tenor of the tale, and closely parallels a verse from a Scottish ballad of comparable antiquity and stature, 'Lord Thomas and Fair Eleanor', where it self-evidently fits:

> She dressed herself in silk so fine,
> Her waiting maids in green,
> And every town that she rode through
> They took her to be some queen.[11]

It may have originally been intended to follow on from a verse found in

110

Buchan's version:

> She's drawn the slippers on her feet,
> Were covered o'er wi' gold,
> Well lined wi' velvet fine,
> To had her frae the cold.[12]

This verse appears in the eighteenth century English broadside, though not in the American broadside. The gold and velvet slippers, also in Motherwell G, are intended to be part of the dæmonic spirit's array of enticements. On the other hand, the carpenter's wife parading through town serves no obvious plot function (many American versions containing this verse have lost the rhyme of 'gold', reverting to a second couplet as per 'Lord Thomas & Fair Eleanor'). Presumably the verse served a didactic purpose, one at odds with the non-moralizing popular ballad advocated by Mr. Graves, i.e. pride before the fall. As Dave Harker has written, in reference to 'James Harris', "quite why the carpenter should be sorry to lose such an apparently capricious wife ... is not made clear."[13]

And yet the carpenter's wife's passage through town has been the most enduring Scottish motif - where it is absent from American tradition the story has usually been curtailed by memory loss. However, American versions have distorted a Scottish original to such an extent that, according to one authority, the verse quoted above (Note 10) is "not directly related to anything in Child [though] it evidently evolved from E8."[14] E8 reads:

> As they were walking up the street,
> Most beautiful for to behold,
> He cast a glamour o'er her face,
> And it shone like the brightest gold.[15]

Quite how the Davies A verse evolved from Motherwell's E8 without being related, I know not. As close an approximation as it is to Motherwell, Davies A8 has not so much evolved, as devolved. Motherwell's third line makes the nuance of the verse accord with Buchan's, i.e. the diabolic spirit has not simply enticed her with promises, he has actually enchanted her away. In his glossary, Child defines

111

'glamour' as "a charm deluding the eye," but, on the strength of its far
more renowned use in 'The Gypsy Laddie', it has some hypnotic
connotation that implies a lot more than 'charm'. The phrase 'under his
spell' seems to befit its meaning best, particularly when applied to
Johnny Fa, the original gypsy laddie:

> She came trippin' down the stair,
> And her nine maidens afore her;
> But up and starts him Johnny Fa,
> And he cast the glamour o'er her.[16]

A phrase like "cast the glamour o'er her" would soon be lost on a New
World singer. As 'Johnny Fa' became 'Gypsy Davy' it was quickly
supplanted by the resolutely rational, "charmed the heart of a lady." One
presumes a similar process occured in 'The House Carpenter', resulting
in either the verse falling off the song (it was evidently absent from De
Marsan's source) or - like as not - becoming a reflection not of the
dæmon lover's powers but the carpenter's wife's vanity, as the focus of
the ballad began to shift in the lady's direction, making her mindset
American singers' primary concern.

That a verse like this should have displayed such tenacity within
American tradition, obdurately rebutting even De Marsan's black talons,
suggests some very entrenched roots. It seems inconceivable, without
its own broadside imprint, that this verse could occur in the majority of
complete American texts unless it had become very firmly established in
American tradition pre-De Marsan.

The link between this verse and the 'hills of heaven and hell' is also
reasonably solid. Not only do they appear together in Motherwell (E), but
most American texts to feature 'the hills of heaven and hell' also contain
the 'glittering like gold' verse, vestiges (presumably) of a once buoyant
supernatural tradition enduring in America's backwaters. Whether this
tradition was already wilting before the advent of American print one can
only hazard a guess.

What the preponderance of the 'glittering like gold' verse in Stateside
tradition is not about to reveal is the antiquity of our ballad. For that, we
must return to the 'hills of heaven and hell', the starting point of our

quest. Thankfully, though Scottish tradition has yielded a fraction over naught in the way of 'modern' texts, we do have more than a couple of dozen examples from American tradition with which to construct a picture of the original drama played out in these lines.

In Scott "the sun shines sweetly on" the hills of heaven, while the mountains of hell are "dreary wi' frost and snow." In Motherwell E - which I have suggested may provide a more authentic denouement than Scott - the hill of heaven "shines so clear to see," while the hill of hell "looks so dark to me." Neither version is entirely convincing (Scott appears to be alone in making mountains out of hills). The mark of Scott - i.e. his mountains of hell and the devil striking "the tap-mast wi' his hand" - has failed to impact on tradition a single jot, despite the popularity of the many editions of his *Minstrelsy* (the 1972 *Kentucky Folklore* published a text derived from Scott, though there is no evidence of passage through oral tradition). Evidently the dæmon strain of the ballad had already been transmitted to America by the time Scott unleashed his text on the world.

Though traces of Scottish origin have been eradicated from many a traditional American rendition, the 'hills of heaven and hell' crop up on a number of Stateside performances, albeit a marked minority among the two hundred and twenty-plus versions collected in America. Of the thirty-two American renditions referenced (see appendix), not one accords with Motherwell or Scott in the particulars. And yet two what-might-be-deemed-unifying features bind these versions:
(i) almost without exception the description of the hills of heaven and hell revolves around 'white as snow' and 'black as a crow'.
(ii) around three-quarters of the versions that survive in some fulsome state also feature the 'glittering like gold' verse.

The standard American version, where it appears, seems to have been surprisingly consistent:

> Oh, what is that [hill] that shines so white,
> That shines as white as snow?
> Oh, those are the hills of heaven itself,
> Where we may never go.

113

Oh, what is that [hill] that shines so black,
That shines as black as a crow?
Oh, that is the [hills] of Hell itself,
Where you and I must go.[17]

The existence of around thirty renditions containing an obvious debt to a Scottish original, and yet consistent in their departure from that source (whether Motherwell or Scott come closest to the original strain), raises some interesting questions.

Before following the trail back to Scotland, perhaps one should examine any American alternatives to the snow/crow duopoly that contain traditional credentials. Just four reject both snow and crow, two from John Cox's collecting, one in Mellinger E. Henry's *Folk-Songs From The Southern Highlands*, and a recording by Jean Ritchie (which I largely discount on the grounds that Ritchie comes from the 'creative' school of traditional folksinger). In Cox's 1938 collection, *Traditional Ballads Mainly From West Virginia*, comes a version that contrasts hills "bright and green" with those "so rough and steep," probably the result of embellished amnesia taking over from tradition.

An earlier Cox text, the A text to his 1925 collection *Folk-Songs Of The South*, accords well with Henry's. Both come close to Motherwell's "so dark to me" with their hills "bright and high" and "dark and low" (cf. Van Ronk). Henry's C text has "so bright above" and hills "so dark below," as does Charles Morrow Wilson's *Backwoods America*, though Wilson's text accords so closely with Henry's that - coming from an uncited source in the same area Henry collected in - I have not considered it a source unto itself. However, four other American renditions refer to hills "dark and low" (or, in one significant fragment's case, "dark as driven woe"), one of which proves to be Clay Walters' 'ship carpenter' text (discussed in chapter two). Given collection in Arkansas, Kentucky, Virginia and Tennessee these handful of 'alternates' probably represent a subsidiary strain *of transatlantic origin*. However, even these four versions preserve the allusion to 'white as snow'.

Of course, the 'snow/crow' dichotomy could be purely American, hence its absence from our two nineteenth-century Scottish texts. Er, no. As it happens, a fortuitous discovery, a 'new' text of 'The Dæmon Lover', collected, remarkably enough, in 1960, forces us to return even these lines to Scotland. The rendition in question, collected by Hamish Henderson in Blairgowrie, Perthshire, was sung by one Andrew Stewart, who said he had learnt it from his mother. Though he had a tune, in common-time (4/4), Mr. Stewart recollected just two verses and the vaguest of outlines. Speaking first, he recalled:

This was another of my mother's songs - a woman was running away with a man ... she was in the boat ... saw a mountain ... says to the man in the boat (the Devil) ... says,

> (sung)
> What hill, what hill is thon I see,
> As white as any snow?
> Oh thon is the hill of Heaven, he said,
> Where all good people go.
>
> What hill, what hill is thon I see,
> As black as any crow?
> Thon is the hill of Hell, he said,
> Where you and I must go.[18]

So 'The Dæmon Lover' existed in Scottish tradition a generation ago. Though these are very much the autumn leaves of tradition, they confirm that even these images originated in Britain (I think we can discount the possibility of the fragment in question crossing back over the Atlantic, particularly as Mr Stewart confirms the man as the Devil, an association made but once in American tradition). That this particular duality (snow/crow) has a more authentic pedigree than the examples of Motherwell and Scott is surely borne out by the range and consistency of their appearance in America. For variants to have been collected from the Ozarks to the Appalachians, and for these verses to have survived the debilitating impact of the broadside/s (almost every version betrays some textual relayering at the hand of De Marsan), a series of British renditions - from a common source - *must* have established themselves early in American tradition, only to be overtaken, as Shakespeare so eloquently put it, by "a ballad in print o' life."

(x) "The hills of heaven and hell"

Ballads ... have found their themes, to which they have given a colour strongly original, in popular tradition, in previous poems, in the romances of chivalry, in real events, and often in the imaginations of their authors, nourished by beliefs, superstitions, and reminiscences of all kinds current in a society where civilisation is scarcely yet established, and numerous vestiges still subsist of the barbarism and paganism that preceded Christianity - Gaston Paris.[1]

The 'James Harris' broadside proves that our song was extant and its revenant nature explicit at the time of the English Civil War. Yet, given that the 'hills of heaven and hell' verses were not first collected until 1803, and that such a dialogue is absent from both English broadsides, the antique provenance I've ascribed to these verses may still strike the reader as largely speculative, based as it is on circumstantial evidence that these verses crossed over to America with the first wave of Scottish emigrants, probably in the early eighteenth century. Thankfully, these verses also contain clues that the ballad has roots as far back as the fifteenth century:

> What hill, what hill is thon I see,
> As white as any snow?
> Oh thon is the hill of Heaven, he said,
> Where all good people go.
>
> What hill, what hill is thon I see,
> As black as any crow?
> Thon is the hill of Hell, he said,
> Where you and I must go.[2]

As is often the case in tradition, these verses allude to others found in Scottish balladry. Indeed the allusion is found in a ballad I had known for many years prior to Sony's belated release of Dylan's 'House Carpenter' in 1991. Recorded by Steeleye Span, the most successful English folk-rock band of the seventies - who presumably learnt it from Ewan MacColl's 1956 Riverside recording - 'Thomas the Rhymer' drew directly from a venerable tradition revolving around Scotland's most famous seer, a thirteenth century prophet by the name of Thomas of Erceldoune. Thomas the Rhymer - as he became known because of his rhyming prophecies - is a shadowy figure in Scottish history. Though his visage loomed large through the fourteenth, fifteenth and sixteenth centuries, very little is known about Thomas save the swirl of legend. This legend sprung up with some rapidity, maintaining a determined hold on Scottish lore down through the centuries.

Thomas came to popular hero status at much the same time as the even more shadowy figure of Robin Hood was allegedly frequenting parts of Sherwood and/or Barnsdale forests. However, he was not, as Child asserts Hood was, "absolutely a creation of the ballad-muse."[3]

Unlike Robin Hood, we can be 100% sure that Thomas of Erceldoune was a real historic character, even if historical particulars are few. We know that Thomas's son, who nominated himself 'Thomas of Ercildoun, son and heir of Thomas Rymour of Ercildoun', disposed of family land in 1299, while Thomas's name is on a deed that probably dates from the 1230s or 1240s, suggesting that the elder Thomas was probably born around 1210 and died sometime shortly before his son's dispersal of land. By 1306, his prophecies were already being alluded to by Barbour:

> I hope that Thomas's prophesie,
> Of Erceldoun, shall truly be.[4]

The 'Whole Prophecie' of Merlin, Thomas Rymour &c. were still being 'collected' and issued as a chapbook as late as 1603. According to Robert Chambers, even in his day (1870) the common people of Scotland continued to regard Thomas's prophecies with veneration "and to preserve a great number of his prophetic sayings."[5]

Though Thomas was no "creation of the ballad-muse" it was inevitable that folklore surrounding the man would become ballad lore in turn. Though he was not a Scottish Robin Hood, he *was* someone popular minstrels were bound to sing about, reflecting an idealized vision of manhood. How many ballads arose because of the legend, or were affected by it, we do not know. Most would have arisen at the very birth of the ballad form, i.e. the tip-end of the fourteenth and into the fifteenth centuries, at the same time as the Robin Hood ballads first began proliferating in England. However, a sixteenth century nursery song, 'Thom a Lin', may once have had life as a narrative ballad, while a variant of the ancient ballad 'Earl Brand', entitled 'Erlinton', was also once known as 'True Tammas' (Child 8B), Thomas the Rhymer's other common moniker. And two important ballads relating the adventures of True Tammas *have* been preserved, 'Thomas the Rhymer' and 'Tam Lin', both betraying medieval origins.

In ballad terms, the part of Thomas's life that seems to have inspired the popular imagination is the seven years he allegedly spent as lover to the Queen of Fairies, and his attendant acquisition of prophetic powers, which Sir Walter Scott described in these terms:

> **Whatever doubts ... the learned might have [had], as to the source of the Rhymer's prophetic skill, the vulgar had no hesitation to ascribe the whole to the intercourse between the bard and the Queen of Faery. The popular tale bears, that Thomas was carried off, at an early age, to the Fairy Land, where he acquired all the knowledge, which made him afterwards so famous. According to the popular belief, he still 'drees his weird' in Fairy Land, and is one day expected to revisit earth.[6]**

This legend first found the page as a metrical romance. A work entitled 'Incipit Prophesia Thomæ de Erseldoun' exists "in four somewhat defective copies: the earliest written a little before the middle of the fifteenth century, two others about 1450, the fourth later."[7] This 66-verse romance was presumably intended for performance, quite possibly to a set tune. Such medieval romances were frequently 'sung' to a harp accompaniment. The anonymous early fourteenth century English romance, 'Sir Orfeo', opens with a declaration that implies it was the norm to 'sing' such romances:

> We often read and written find,
> as learned men do us remind,
> that lays that now the harpers sing
> are wrought of many a marvellous thing ...
> In Britain all these lays are writ,
> there issued first in rhyming fit,
> concerning adventures in those days
> whereof the Britons made their lays;

for when they heard men anywhere
tell of adventures that there were,
they took their harps in their delight
and made a lay and named it right.
Of adventures that did once befall
some can tell you, but not all.
Listen now, lordings, good and true,
and 'Orfeo' I will sing to you.[8]

The survival of four fifteenth century manuscripts of the romance of Thomas suggests it probably enjoyed a period of sustained popularity in the Middle Ages, though at this point in time it would have been the sole preserve of the professional minstrel, whose responsibilities and privileges were still as delineated as any medieval caste ("We willing to restrain ... outrageous enterprises and idleness, have ordained that to the houses of prelates, earls, and barons, none resort to meat and drink, unless he be a minstrel." - Proclamation of Edward II, 1316[9]).

As Child notes, the romance refers twice to an older source - "als the storye tellis full ryghte" [i.e. as the story tells us right well] and "gyff it be als the storye sayes" [i.e. if it be as the story says][10]. He was of the opinion that the older story, "was undoubtedly a romance which narrated the adventure of Thomas with the elf queen *simply*, without specification of his prophecies. In all probability it concluded, in accordance with the ordinary popular tradition, with Thomas's return to fairyland after a certain time passed in this world."[11] As it happens, what we have in ballad-form are two quite different accounts of Thomas's time in fairyland. We have no guarantees that this older story, if it ever existed save in the popular imagination, did not depart from the romance when it came to the means of Thomas's escape from fairyland - the point of divergence for our two ballads.

The metrical romance 'Thomas off Ersseldoune' was unquestionably the source for one of the ballads in question, 'Thomas the Rhymer'. The visions the Queen of the Fairies shows to Thomas in the romance should have a familiar ring.:

Sees thou, Thomas, yon fayr way,   *See thou now the fair way,*

119

That lygges ouyr yone fayr playn?	*That lies over yon high mountain?*
Yonder is the way to heuyn for ay,	*That is the way to heaven for all,*
Whan synful sawles haf derayed their payne	*When sinful souls end their pain.*
Sees thou, Thomas, yon second way,	*See thou now the second way*
That lygges lawe undir the ryse?	*That lies low under the rise?*
Streight is the way sothly to say,	*Straight is the way, forsooth to say,*
To the joys of paradyce.	*To the joys of paradise.*
Sees thou, Thomas, yon thyrd way,	*But see thou now yon third way,*
That ligges ouyr yone [deep dell]?	*That lies over yon deep dell?*
Wide is the way sothly to say	*That is the way, so alas!*
To the brynyng fyres of hell.[12]	*Unto the burning fire of hell.*

However, it is very unlikely that the anonymous author of (or interpolator to) 'The Dæmon Lover' took as his/her source the metrical romance, even if the romance enjoyed a limited currency into the sixteenth century. An intermediary process, which cut the sixty-six verse romance to a third of its length, also made it conform to a new, increasingly populist, ballad form. Whereas in the metrical romance the Queen shows Thomas four paths, the fourth of which is the one to Elfland, in the ballad of 'Thomas the Rhymer' True Thomas is only shown three paths:

> O see not ye yon narrow road,
> So thick beset wi' thorns and briers?
> That is the path of righteousness,
> Tho' after it but few enquires.
>
> And see not ye that braid braid road,
> That lies across yon lillie leven?
> That is the path of wickedness,
> Tho' some call it the road to heaven.
>
> And see not ye that bonny road,
> Which winds about the fernie brae?
> That is the road to fair Elfland,
> Whe[re] you and I this night maun gae.[13]

Though the final line is the only verbatim 'lift', the whole tenor of the two verses in 'The Dæmon Lover' betray a debt to 'Thomas the Rhymer'. In Clay Walter's rendition, he actually designates "the hills of heaven" as a place "where all righteous people go." If it remains hard to conceive how verses from such a strange source could be the inspiration for those in 'The Dæmon Lover', one corrupted two-verse fragment of the latter, collected in Virginia in March 1914, perhaps provides a single word residue of motherland tradition connecting the hills of heaven directly to Thomas's path of righteousness:

> See those fairy banks of heaven
> White as driven snow?
> They are the fairy banks of heaven
> Where you and I can't go.
>
> See those cloudy banks of heaven
> Dark as driven woe?
> They are the cloudy banks of torment
> Where you and I shall go.[14]

Given such a clear debt, when did it occur? Scottish literary critic T.F. Henderson would like us to believe that the reworking of the romance into 'Thomas the Rhymer' was "a comparatively modern concoction"[15]. David C. Fowler, in his 1968 book *A Literary History Of The Popular Ballad*, makes the even more extraordinary suggestion that 'Thomas the Rhymer' was probably composed by Mrs. Brown of Falkland (1747-1810), whose husband was the minister at Falkland and whose father was professor at King's College, Aberdeen, and from whom the earliest surviving text was relayed to Walter Scott and Robert Jamieson.

Neither Henderson's nor Fowler's position is really tenable. For 'Thomas the Rhymer' to be based upon a fifteenth century metrical romance and yet be a seventeenth or eighteenth century "concoction" begs a simple retort: where would said author have obtained a copy of the romance? It had long fallen out of circulation, and was not published until Scott and Jamieson included different texts as a reference-aid to 'Thomas the Rhymer'. Neither can such a recent authorship explain the excellent text communicated to Scott in 1806 by one Christiana Greenwood of

London, "from the recitation of her mother and her aunt, both then above sixty, who learned it in their childhood from Kirstan Scot, a very old woman, at Longnewton, near Jedburgh."[16]

Condensing a metrical romance is hardly the sort of literary exercise that an eighteenth century wannabe balladeer might choose to embark upon. On the other hand, the 'condensed metrical romance', on the considerable evidence of the 550-page Percy folio ms. (probably compiled largely from popular minstrel sources), was once an entire genre of traditional balladry, reflecting the rapid demographic shifts in the popular minstrels' audience in the late fifteenth and sixteenth centuries (put crudely, from gentry to yeoman to tavern). These 'condensed metrical romances' seem to have been the last gasp of the popular minstrel - hence, a short-lived phenomenon. Child included three such ballads in *English & Scottish Popular Ballads* - 'The Boy and the Mantle', 'King Arthur and King Cornwall', and 'The Marriage of Sir Gawain' - but admitted himself, in his introduction to the first of these:

> **This ballad and the two which follow it are clearly not of the same rise, and not meant for the same ears, as those which go before. They would come down by professional rather than by domestic tradition, through minstrels rather than knitters and weavers. They suit the hall better than the bower, the tavern or public square better than the cottage, and would not go to the spinning-wheel at all.**[17]

We are almost entirely beholden to the Percy folio - a wide-ranging ms. compiled in the mid-seventeenth century, largely from sixteenth century sources, rescued from the beckoning oblivion of a friend's fireplace by Bishop Percy - for evidence that this was a significant intermediary stage separating the metrical romance from the popular ballad or, as Mr. Graves would have it, "the ballad proper."

But perhaps the aspersions of Fowler and Henderson can only be definitively dismissed by considering all the evidence of traditional interaction between the two Thomas Rhymer ballads - 'Thomas the Rhymer' and 'Tam Lin' - something that can only have occured over a substantial passage of time.

The close relationship between 'Tam Lin' and 'Thomas the Rhymer'

(Child Ballads 39 and 37 respectively) is something of which Child himself remained steadfastly unaware. Missing the significance of an allusion to Thomas the Rhymer in a version of 'Tam Lin' in an October 1818 issue of *The Scots Magazine,* he notes that Thomas the Rhymer "appears in the last lines with very great distinction, but it is not clear what part he has in the story."[18] The lines in question are:

> Four an twenty noble kings
> Cam by on steeds o snaw,
> But True Thomas, the gude Rhymer,
> Was king outower them a'.[19]

Child chose to pass over the obvious inference, that 'True Thomas' *was* 'Tam Lin'. Nor is this by any means the only instance of 'Tam Lin' and 'Thomas the Rhymer' interacting in tradition. Indeed, even the 'paths to heaven and hell' have been known to cross this particular divide.

'Thomas the Rhymer' was collected just three times by Scott in the early nineteenth century (though Mrs Brown's rendition, part of the Tytler-Brown ms., actually dates from 1783), and a single time at the turn of the twentieth (in a new guise), always in Scotland. No earlier text has survived. As such, its relationship with the metrical romance is the only real clue as to its antiquity. Thankfully, we are not so beholden to supposition to confirm the antiquity of 'Tam Lin', which has a pedigree stretching through five hundred years of reasonably solid Scottish tradition.

'Tam Lin' is a, perhaps the, supreme example of the supernatural ballad as we know it, with key thematic and stylistic traits already in place (of the 24 action-based ballad formulae cited in Andersen's *Commonplace And Creativity*, 'Tam Lin' utilizes no less than nine). Though the record of tunes begins with Burns', the implication of a 1549 document is that it was already something of a stalwart of Scottish tradition. That tradition was something quite separate and distinct from the metrical romance, possibly a more authentic tradition. In 'Tam Lin', the hero convinces a maiden he has seduced into rescuing him from Fairyland, where he had been taken some seven years previously by the Queen of Fairies, lest he ends up as the fairies' septennial tithe to hell:

123

22. "Ance it fell upon a day,
A cauld day and a <u>snell</u>,   *[frost*
When we were frae the hunting come,
That from my horse I fell.

23. "The Queen of Fairies she came by,
Took me wi' her to dwell,
Evn where she has a pleasant land
For those that in it dwell,
But at the end o seven years,
They pay their <u>teind</u> to hell..[20]   *[tithe*

'Thomas the Rhymer' as a separate entity cannot be given the sustained grasp on tradition that assures us it was around long enough to impact on 'The Dæmon Lover'. 'Tam Lin' can. In *The Complaynt Of Scotland*, published anonymously in 1549, the author comes upon some shepherds swopping songs and stories, and itemizes those he can recall. Unfortunately, ballad-titles being an amorphous lot, a degree of interpretation is required to align the Complaynt with recognizable songs, though the key entry is "the tayl of the yo[u]ng tamlene, and of the bald braband" (one presumes "the bald braband" to be a separate song, perhaps 'The Bold Earl Brand').

The significance of *The Complaynt* is that, as a text with an authoritative date, it:
(i) provides something that no previous historical reference to 'ballets', 'ballades', 'rymes' &c. does - song titles.
(ii) gives a sample of ballads and songs in popular currency in the first half of the sixteenth century.

The other identifiable ballads cited in *The Complaynt* suggest ones long dipped in the stream of tradition, i.e. a Robin Hood ballad ('Robin Hood and Little John' could be any of the known early Robin Hood ballads), 'The Hunting of the Cheviot' and 'The Battle of Otterburn', both dealing with the 1388 Scots triumph, and a ballad about the 1411 Battle of Harlaw. So does the 'Tam Lin' that has come down to us accord with this "tayl of the yo[u]ng tamlene"?

If Robert Burns and Sir Walter Scott both published versions of 'Tam

Lin', in each case their primary source was the same manuscript, though Burns probably knew the ballad himself from tradition. He did, after all, provide a tune, and Child cites Burns' *Musical Museum* text as, "the only version which has preserved an essentially correct [transformation] process: Tam Lin, when a burning gleed, is to be thrown into well-water, from which he will step forth a naked knight."[21]

If Child is correct then Burns was thoroughly conversant with the song. However, the version of 'Tam Lin' on which Burns was [otherwise] reliant can be found in an eighteenth century manuscript compiled by his friend Robert Riddell, housed at Glenriddell House. The quality of this text, its lack of narrative holes and sophisticated use of triple-rhyming couplets (see over) pretty much requires us to suppose that Riddell's 'Tam Lin' is no late eighteenth century transcription from oral tradition, but an altogether more authentic text, perhaps from a manuscript source. T.F. Henderson states as much in his general study, *The Ballad In Literature*, calling the Glenriddell text of 'Tam Lin' "a wonderfully good version of this ballad," but doubting it is one that had been greatly exposed to popular tradition:

> **The original authority for the Glenriddell version is quite unknown; but, if given exactly as 'preserved by tradition', that tradition could hardly have been a popular one, for both the rhythm and the rhyme are remarkably good, and there is hardly a trace of vulgarization, either in idea or language.[22]**

Robert Riddell (1755-94) was an antiquarian, not a ballad-collector per se. The ballads comprise (a small) part of Riddell's twelve-volume "Collection of Scottish Antiquities." 'Tam Lin' is unique among the fifteen ballads in the ms. in that it appears in volume eight of the collection, with a date of 1789. The remaining ballads all appear in volume eleven, with a date of 1791 (including a second notation of 'Tam Lin', containing more notes). The full title given in the Glenriddell ms. is, "An Old Song Called Young Tom Line." Suffice to say, it is the only item specifically prefixed, "An Old Song..." and the use of Young Tom Line (with a silent 'e' and a long 'i'?) appears to be unique to Riddell.[23]

Presuming that Riddell's 'Tam Lin' corresponds with the "tayl" sung by the shepherds in *The Complaynt Of Scotland*, its original audience would have been in no doubt as to the identity of 'True Tammas' (just as they would have known that 'The Hunting of the Cheviot' was an allegorical version of the Battle of Otterburn). Given the kinship of the two ballads, 'Thomas the Rhymer' and 'Tam Lin' might even have been intended to be performed together, telling first the tale of Thomas's capture by the Queen of the Fairies and the visions she showed him, and then his escape from Fairyland (which 'Thomas the Rhymer' does not concern itself with, save for a possibly interpolated final verse).

Neither 'Tam Lin' nor 'Thomas the Rhymer' have lent themselves to the processes of rationalization. They have remained obdurately Scottish in transmission, not once making the trip through American tradition (Dorothy Scarborough collected a rendition in 1932 but from a first generation Scot). It is tempting to view the sensibilities of these two ballads - the combination of redemption through love, rivalry, magic, mystery and courtly grace - as a peculiarly Scottish combination.

In 'Tam Lin', Thomas's departure from fairyland has become necessary because every seven years the queen of the fairies must pay a tithe to hell (see verse 23). The Greenwood version of 'Thomas the Rhymer' (given to Scott in 1806) likewise contains a warning to Thomas from the queen of the fairies:

> Ilka seven years, Thomas,
> We pay our teindings unto hell,
> And ye're sae leesome and sae strang
> That I fear, Thomas, it will be yeresell.[24]

Though Mrs. Brown omits this verse from her more famous rendition, it parallels lines in the metrical romance, and therefore presumably derives from the original strain of 'Thomas the Rhymer':

Tomorrowe of helle ye foule fende	*Tomorrow the foulest fiend of hell*
Amang our folke shall chuse his fee;	*Shall exact his tithe from our people*
For you art a larg man and an hende,	*And because you are a large and noble man*
Trowe you wele he will chuse thee.[25]	*Mark my words! He will choose thee.*

The only span of time mentioned in the romance, however, is "three yere and more."[26] Clearly, somewhere in the winding ways of tradition,

'Thomas the Rhymer' interacted with 'Tam Lin'. The seven-year span reoccurs in all four versions of 'Thomas the Rhymer' that appear in Child (including his misassigned 39M). Even the one variant of 'Thomas the Rhymer' to have been collected in the last hundred years - a remarkable 25-verse version gathered by Dr. Shearer, headmaster at Gordon Schools, Huntly, at the turn of the century, and published in *The Huntly Express* as 'Sir John Gordon' (Thomas's newly-acquired identity) - has several references to the term he must remain with the queen, including this memorable verse:

> My dear Sir John, my bonnie Sir John,
> Since ye hae kissed me,
> Through weal and woe, as it may chance,
> Seven years my slave ye maun be.[27]

Sadly, Shearer's version does not feature any 'paths to heaven and hell'. Nor is it known whether 'Sir John Gordon' enjoyed a healthy life in tradition as a separate entity - much as 'Henry Martyn', though clearly derived from 'Sir Andrew Barton', managed to retain an independent existence.

As has already been mentioned, the seven-year term once held considerable significance. Robert Graves puts a persuasive case in *English & Scottish Ballads* that the tithe to hell really referred to Hecate, who required "a sturdy man or boy once every seven years."[28] This certainly ties in with Thomas's supposed physique, "a larg man and an hende." In 'Tam Lin', though, True Thomas is saved not *by* the Queen but against her express wishes. Indeed, she cries out in anguish:

> 'But had I kend, Tam Lin,' she says,
> 'What now this night I see,
> I wad hae taen out thy twa grey een,
> And put in twa een o' tree.'[29]

The Queen's cry need not necessarily be one of romantic anguish. It may well reflect a genuine fear that Thomas would reveal the secrets of the fairies, a fear that manifests itself in our twentieth century variant of 'Thomas the Rhymer', 'Sir John Gordon', as an out-and-out threat:

127

> Fareweel, fareweel, my noble lord,
> Your promise you've kept to me;
> But mine ye maun be if ye tell on earth
> What here ye did hear or see.[30]

It still surprises me that Child did not recognize 'Tam Lin' and 'Thomas the Rhymer' as sharing more than a common motif or two, even after he gained access to the Abbotsford material. Nor did he seemingly consider the possibility that 'Tam Lin' might represent not merely a parallel, but a parent tradition, from which the author of the fourteenth century romance himself may have freely borrowed.

What evidence is there tying the tale of 'Tam Lin' to Thomas of Erceldoune, if one discounts his kidnapping by fairies, on the grounds that such things happened all the time in olden days? The most convincing evidence is the name itself. In the various collected renditions the hero's name is rarely Tam Lin. In the Glenriddell ms. it is Tom, though both Janet and the Queen call him Thomas. In Herd's fragment, the earliest collected, which he calls 'Kertonha, or, The Fairy Court' ('Kertonha' appearing to be an oral corruption of Carterhaugh, "a wooded peninsula at confluence of the Ettrick and Yarrow, two and a quarter miles south-west of Selkirk"), he is simply Thomas. In Buchan, he *is* called Tam-a-Line, but always 'True Tam-a-Line'. He is called 'True Thomas' in Child's K text, communicated to Scott by Hugh Irvine in 1812, and 'Thomas' in Child's M text, communicated to Scott in 1802.

Moving to the early twentieth century, we find an excellent (though, sadly, tuneless) 45-verse text for 'Tam Lin' collected by Gavin Greig from that first class repository of balladry, Miss Bell Robertson, in which 'Tam Lin' is identified throughout as 'True Tammas'. The association of 'Tam Lin' with True Thomas was evidently no one transmitter's whim. True Thomas is also the way the hero is identified in all three versions of 'Thomas the Rhymer' collected by Scott. Robert Graves even has an ingenious theory why the name 'True Thomas' came to apply to Thomas of Erceldoune:

> Taking a sudden fancy to Thomas, whom [the Queen] met when out hunting, she introduced him to her secret Court, and announced that he had already taken the necessary oath to her under the elder-tree, this

being a tree which symbolised death in the Old Religion ... Green was the witches' uniform - hence Robin Hood's Lincoln green, and the green sleeve of the Maid of Slane. The Queen of Elphame wore it, and made Thomas wear it too. Nine bells hung from her horse's mane because nine was the number sacred to the all-wise Moon-goddess Hecate ... Converts to the Old Religion had to abjure Christianity, be tattooed with a secret mark, and accept new baptismal names or nicknames. Thus ... Thomas became 'True Thomas'.[31]

Mr. Graves, like Professor Child, did not make the connection between 'Tam Lin' and 'Thomas the Rhymer' and therefore - though he may well have had the right idea - I suspect he applied the wrong name. True Thomas was surely a moniker intended to reflect the Rhymer's duly acquired prophetic powers. The disenchantment of Tam Lin, on the other hand, may lead us to an explanation of *this* curious name. In his highly influential *The Magic Arts In Celtic Britain* (1945), Lewis Spence wrote of the ritual Thomas undergoes to escape fairyland:

[One] theory [is] that people taken to the Fairie[s] were actually believed to have undergone some process analogous to death which, in a special and primitive sense, signified a transformation into animal form, and that Tamlane must naturally reverse this process and repass through the animal and other forms which man was thought of as assuming subsequent to his death ... During the process of disenchantment Janet must keep continually calling out the hero's name. Is Tamlane the hero's otherworld name? It has been suggested that by giving him an unearthly name the elves have cut him off from human converse ... In one version of the ballad we [even] read:

First they did call me Jack, he said,
And then they called me John,
But since I lived in the fairy court
Tamlane has always been my name.[32]

Now a question swirling around thy cranium at this point may well be: damnably interesting as all this is, pray tell, what has it to do with the origins of 'The House Carpenter'? The answer is that the author of 'The Dæmon Lover' - if the hills of heaven and hell derive from its original template, as I am inclined to believe - was either conversant with 'Thomas the Rhymer' or even, possibly, an ancient version of 'Tam Lin' that incorporated elements of 'Thomas the Rhymer'.

For evidence that such an amalgam existed one must turn to a version of 'Tam Lin' sent by Major Hutton to Walter Scott in December 1802, after he had read the first volume of Scott's *Minstrelsy Of The Scottish Border* (in which Scott had printed his 'Tale of Tamlane'). In his letter, Major Hutton intimates that stanzas 46-49 of Scott's version should be struck out and the following verses inserted. But the verses in question do not 'belong' to 'Tam Lin':

1. My father was a noble knight,
And was much gi'n to play,
And I myself a bonny boy,
And followed him away.

2. He rowd me in his hunting-coat
And layd me down to sleep,
And by the queen of fairies came,
And took me up to keep.

3. She set me on a milk-white steed;
'T was o' the elfin kind;
His feet were shot wi' beaten goud,
And fleeter than the wind.

4. Then we raid on and on'ard mair,   *[more*
O'er mountain, hill and lee   *[untilled ground*
Till we came to a hie, hie wa',
Upon a mountain's bree.   *[brow*

5. The apples hung like stars of goud
Out-our that wa' sa fine;
I put my hand to pu' down ane,   *[one*
For want of food I thought to tine.

6. O had your hand, Tamas! she said,
O let that evil fruit now be!

It was that apple ye see there
Beguil'd man and woman in your country.

**7. O dinna ye see yon road, Tamas,
Down by yon lilie lee?
Blessed is the man who yon gate gaes,
It leads him to the heavens hie.**

**8. And dinna ye see yon road, Tamas,
Down by yon frosty fell?
Curst is the man that yon gate gaes,
For it leads to the gates of hell.**

9. O dinna ye see yon castle, Tamas,
That's biggit between the twa,
And theekit wi' the beaten goud?
O that's the fairies' ha'.

10. O when ye come to the ha', Tamas,
See that a weel-learnd boy ye be;
They'll ask ye questions ane and a',
But see ye answer nane but me.

11. If ye speak to ain but me, Tamas,
A fairie ye maun ever bide;
But if ye speak to nane but me, Tamas,

Ye may come to be your country's pride.

12. And when he came to Fairie Ha,
I wot a weel-learned boy was he;
They askd him questions ane and a',
But he answered nane but his ladie.

13. There was four-and-twenty gude
knights'-sons
In fairie land obliged to bide,
And of a' the pages that were there
Fair Tamas was his ladie's pride.

14. There was four-and-twenty earthly boys,
Wha all played at the ba,
But Tamas was the bonniest boy,
And playd the best amang them a'.

15. There was four-and-twenty earthly maids,
Wha' a' playd at the chess,
Their colour rosy-red and white,
Their gowns were green as grass.

16. And pleasant are our fairie sports,
We flie o'er hill and dale;
But at the end of seven years
They pay the <u>teen</u> to hell.   *[tithe*

17. And now's the time, at Hallowmass,
Late on the morrow's even,
And if ye miss me them, Janet,
I'm lost for yearis seven.[33]

As Scott realized, verses 1-16 - which include the 'paths of heaven and hell' - do not constitute part of 'Tam Lin' but rather comprise an edited 'Thomas the Rhymer'. The confusion of names, the seven-year tenure in fairyland and this composite text (presumably part of a much longer 'Tam Lin') all suggest constant interaction through the ages, even the possibility that the verses in question may have attached themselves to

131

some kind of 'True Tammas' composite for a couple of centuries before being passed on to Scott. Major Hutton's version, like Greenwood's, probably represents a strain stretching back to the days of popular minstrelsy - the reference in verse nine to the fairy-castle reflects a passage in the metrical romance unreplicated in the Greenwood or Brown texts.

This all points to 'Thomas the Rhymer' having been 'composed' no later than the sixteenth century. It is hard to conceive of something in this intermediary genre coming much later given the fast-receding opportunities for reciting even a 22-verse condensed-romance. Like 'The Dæmon Lover', it had all but disappeared from Scottish tradition by the end of the eighteenth century. If it were not for Mrs. Brown of Falkland and Mrs Christiana Greenwood, both of whom learnt the song from aged female relatives, no reasonably complete text would be extant (the version in the Campbell ms. and Major Hutton's rendition are at least a dozen verses to the bad). The existence of a 'modern' variant like 'Sir John Gordon' - in which True Thomas is no more, nor the paths of heaven and hell - seems to confirm that its parent-form, 'Thomas the Rhymer', had long faded from tradition.

'Tam Lin', despite its epic length, has survived in Scottish tradition into the twentieth century, perhaps the only genuine Scottish survivor from the age of popular minstrelsy, having transferred successfully to the new repositories of tradition - the "knitters in the sun," as Shakespeare termed them - in the sixteenth century, and been adopted by each generation in turn as the best of conduits back to a mystical past.

'The Dæmon Lover' is unlikely to have been any such product of 'minstrelsy'. It bears all the hallmarks of a new, conciser form of balladry, albeit one that appropriated phrases, lines and even verses from the travelling troubadors of yesteryear - hence, perhaps, the preponderance of ladies in their bowers and reckless knights in these 'new' popular ballads. The 'paths of heaven and hell' - though they never became floating verses - were, like much 'pop' minstrelsy, ripe for rewriting in this new form.

For 'Thomas the Rhymer' and/or 'Tam Lin' to have interacted with 'The Dæmon Lover', inspiring the vision of the 'hills of heaven and hell' -

132

before passage to the likes of North Carolina, Alabama, West Virginia, Kentucky, Florida and Tennessee - they presumably came into contact when the two Thomas ballads were still an integral part of Scottish oral tradition. Realistically, that is unlikely to have been later than the early seventeenth century, i.e. at the cusp between the old and new forms of balladry, professional and amateur. The absence of any allusion to these lines in 'James Harris' denies us concrete evidence that 'The Dæmon Lover' 'always' carried a debt to a fifteenth century source. However, such a debt must have originated in Scotland, irrespective of when it ultimately made its carriage to America.

Once in American tradition, 'The Dæmon Lover' has witnessed an uneven contest between an English broadside upstart and its purer Scottish self, complete with hills of heaven and hell. It has been the overwriting of tradition by a rationalized sibling that has decided this duel. It is hard not to agree with Albert Lord, that the death of oral tradition comes "not when writing is introduced, but when published song texts are spread among singers."[34]

In Scotland all the evidence suggests that 'The Dæmon Lover', like many a product of the golden age of Scottish balladry, was only "flourishing in tradition" until the early eighteenth century, at which point it began to fall rapidly from singers' repertoires. When captured by the Scotts, Buchan, Kinloch and Motherwell it was already becoming subject to uncorrected violent changes. At the same time evidence from underlying "ideological strata" suggests that the ballad proliferated in isolated American communities long before the De Marsan broadside standardized its form, having been transmitted overseas whilst still enjoying full bloom.

The textual evidence of its English life, as with most popular post-folio ballads, can only be found in broadsides. The 'James Harris' text, "contrived into metre" by Laurence Price, strongly suggests by its plot outline that the revenant aspect, though not its original diabolic self, survived the northern marches; that it was rationalized gradually, by omission (a few shavings from these 'ideological strata' remain in the fragments collected from English and Manx tradition). In this it accords with the few other ballads supernatural-in-origin to be collected in England in modern times, reflecting the sort of process that could turn

133

'The Elphin Knight' into 'Scarborough Fair', ensuring that "the riddles have lost their dramatic function, and the story [has become] a straightforward recounting of impossibles, with no challenge from [supernatural] opponents."[35]

The De Marsan broadside - betraying a debt to both eighteenth-century English broadside and Scottish oral tradition - seems to have enjoyed unprecedented dispersal in America. Though it did not introduce 'The House Carpenter' to American tradition (and was evidently taken from recital itself), it seems to have signalled the end of any meaningful oral process, representing as it did "exposure to new and untraditional ways"[36] in a most unwelcome guise. Yet it also ensured that one of the most powerful of Scottish ballads has not gone the way of 'The Battle of Otterburn', 'Childe Waters' or 'The Douglas Tragedy' - into the dustbin of history.

(xi) "Knitters in the sun"

[In the ballads] the Scottish imagination seems to be in revolt against the austerity of Scottish religion. It is the woman, rather than the man, who is in the forefront of the picture. - R.K. Chambers[1]

That Child died before completing (indeed, barely starting) a long-promised general introduction to *English & Scottish Popular Ballads* ensured that a criterion for 'popular balladry' that could embrace 'The Hunting of the Cheviot', 'The Marriage of Sir Gawain', 'The Geste of Robyn Hode', 'The Wee Wee Man', 'Kinmont Willie', 'Judas' and 'Crow and Pie' (which, between them, manage to breach all eight of Graves' criteria for 'the ballad proper'); but exclude 'Young Craigston', 'The Bonnie Lass o' Fyvie' and 'Polly Vaughn' (perhaps better known as 'Young But Daily Growin', 'Pretty Peggy-O' and 'The Shooting of His Dear') was never put to the test. One acid test Child refused to apply was evidence of passage in oral tradition, let alone popular oral tradition (as opposed to transmission by professional minstrels). Yet, as Gerould has pointed out:

> **The popular ballad, the ballad of tradition as I believe we may more justly call it, has no real existence save when held in memory and sung by those who have learned it from the lips of others ... Strictly speaking, the ballad as it exists is not a ballad save when it is in oral circulation, and certainly not until it has been in oral circulation ... An imitation of the ballad style by a lettered poet and a schooled composer, whether made in the fifteenth century or the nineteenth, does not belong to the genre we are considering, though it may be absorbed into the genre by processes of recreation.**[2]

We cannot assume that the Percy folio, say, was compiled from popular sources unless there is external evidence to support candidature. This external evidence need not be an actual post-folio rendition - there are surprisingly few of these: 'King John and the Bishop', 'Childe Waters', 'Glasgerion', 'Childe Maurice', 'Sir Andrew Barton', 'Captain Car' and 'The Heir of Linne' appear to be it. It could be something as left-field as a version of 'The Boy and the Mantle' popping up in a 400-page songbook, *The Charms Of Melody*, published in Dublin in 1818 (this version can be found in Helen Flanders' *Ancient Ballads*).

Should Child have excluded all ballads only extant in pre-eighteenth century manuscripts, lacking corroboration from subsequent oral transmission, he would have been left with barely half a dozen items pre-Folio. 'The Battle of Otterburn' and 'The Hunting of the Cheviot' would still have been entitled to inclusion - in the latter's case because of the sixteenth century broadside derivative, 'Chevy Chase' - as would 'Tam Lin' and 'Thomas the Rhymer'. But out would have had to go several of the finer Robin Hood ballads, and the folio pieces most obviously drawn from minstrelsy - 'King Estmere', all 69 verses, 'Sir John Butler', 'Flodden Field', 'Tom Potts' &c.

And yet if what we are talking about is some genuine form of 'popular balladry' then only minstrel ballads that entered popular tradition (even if duly abbreviated), should entertain a place in the Child canon. That a popular tradition independent of minstrels existed by the early sixteenth century can be attested by the shepherds who sang minstrel-fare in *The Complaynt Of Scotland*. Indeed the 1377 reference in *Piers Plowman* to Sloth knowing "rymes of robyn hode" better than his Paternoster suggests that certain elements of traditional folksong had been in place for quite some time.

That such a tradition took its repertoire from, and remained wholly derivative of, minstrelsy until the end of the fifteenth century seems bourne out by surviving fifteenth century ballads, which invariably include conventions of minstrelsy like the incipit ("Harken, good yeomen, comely, courteous and good..."). The first historical reference to an oral tradition that suggests the choral not the *carole*, the ballad separate from the minstrel, probably comes in an 'Address to the Christian' in 1538 by Miles Coverdale:

> **If women at the rockes [distaffs] and spinnynge at the wheles, had none other songes to pass their tyme withal than such as Moses' sister songe before them, they should be better occupied than with 'Hey, nonny, nonny: Hey, trolly, lolly," and such like fantasies.**[3]

The sixteenth and seventeenth century ballads collected in Scotland that blend'n'blur the activities of revenants, spirits, and other otherworldly intruders do not share the brutishness of the broadside ballads of the day because they sprang from a very different impulse. Should our ballad (and, indeed, 'contemporaneous' works like 'Young Hunting', 'Sweet William's Ghost' &c.) have originated within the group that diseminated it, it could not have been written for any reason other than the simple joy of composition, and the desire to have something to sing. The prospect of anything more than a local fame of sorts would not, could not have been a factor. Such a ballad would have taken a couple of generations or more to achieve anything beyond local notoriety. Yet to have achieved such a widespread dispersal of versions containing even an undercoat of 'original' tradition (a "banks of Italy" here, perhaps a "she shone like glittering gold" there), and to have inspired two popular seventeenth century broadsides, 'The Dæmon Lover' must have enjoyed something akin to national favour in Scotland by the mid-to-late sixteenth century.

But then the level of intelligence of the folk-singing community need not operate in reverse to the level of superstition and belief in the supernatural within that self-same community. Like the majority of popular ballads, 'The Dæmon Lover' was surely composed for the same group/s that chose to sing it, *albeit drawing self-consciously on stylistic conventions formulated over a century and a half of popular minstrelsy*. To suppose that most popular ballads did not derive from the same class of person who chose to preserve them from the ravages of the faddish strikes me as not only unlikely, but quite unjust. Just as a tale of supernatural vengeance, infidelity and temptation, would most likely be written for these "women at the rockes", the most static section of the populace, these themes would also have kept the song alive among ballad-singing womenfolk.

That the form was already thriving by Shakespeare's time can be established by references to the likes of 'Fair Margaret and Sweet William', 'Little Musgrave', 'The Knight and Shepherd's Daughter', 'Dick o' the Cow', and 'The Rose of England' in the plays of Nashe, Shakespeare, Beaumont and Fletcher, and by the appearance of such ballads in the Stationer's Register. Indeed Shakespeare wrote memorably of the genus, minus Coverdale's sanctimony, in *Twelfth*

137

Knight.

> 'tis old and plain;
> The spinners and the knitters in the sun
> And the free maids that weave their thread with bones
> Do use to chant it; it is silly sooth,
> And dallies with the innocence of love.[4]

Evidently spinners and knitters were no longer mere preservers of tradition, but were developing a genuinely popular tradition all their own - at this point perhaps a compendium of scrunched-up ballad-romances, the occasional lachrymose lyric and a type of popular ballad, probably bearing a refrain of the 'hey nonny nonny' or 'the wind blaw my plaid awa' variety.

A contemporary of Shakespeare's, John Deloney, in his 1597 *Pleasant History Of John Winchcomb*, paints a scene for a performance of what Deloney introduces as 'The Maiden's Song' but is better known as Child Ballad No.9, 'The Fair Flower of Northumberland'. In Deloney's portrait:

> **These women, who for the most part were very fair and comely creatures ... were all attired alike from top to toe. Then (after due reverence) the maidens in dulcet manner chanted out this Song, two of them singing the Ditty, and all the rest bearing the burden.[5]**

Presumably the "two ... singing the Ditty," sang alternate verses - perhaps one taking the part of the false knight - making for a quite sophisticated performance. 'The Fair Flower of Northumberland' is a salutary tale of an English lady who releases a Scottish captive from her father's castle and accompanies him across the border, where he announces he is already married and has no further use for her. The moralizing coda, a legacy of the broadside, had clearly already infiltrated popular tradition, the final verse in Deloney reading:

> All you faire maidens be warned by me,
> refrain: Follow, my love, come over the strand,
> Scots were never true, nor never will be,
> refrain: To lord, nor lady, nor faire England.[6]

'The Fair Flower of Northumberland' - which may well be, as Bronson declares, a "libel on the Scottish race"[7] - is also quite different to the mini-epics of yeoman minstrelsy - romantic and didactic, it is a tale of perfidy singularly at odds with the code of courtly honour that had lain at the heart of the medieval metrical romance (if one could establish the pre-existence of 'Lord Bateman' - in which another maiden releases a prisoner in exchange for a promise of marriage - one might even conceive of 'The Fair Flower' as some belated parody). 'The Fair Flower of Northumberland', lending itself to the female perspective as it does, is hardly unique in the annals of popular balladry.

As it is, the one aspect of song we know that the maidens of Coverdale (1538) and Deloney (1597) both adopted was the refrain - evidently once a key component of the 'chants' of these 'knitters in the sun'. Though there has been a debate of sorts about the historical precedence of ballads-with-refrains over ballads-without-refrains - largely because of Grundtvig's now-disparaged premise that as a ballad-type the former took historical precedence - somewhere between little and no work has been done on the types of ballad most likely to utilize a refrain. If refrains were first adopted as a form of communal interplay by womenfolk at work and play, as Deloney strongly implies, one would expect the majority of ballads carrying a burden or refrain to dally "with the innocence of love."

That maids and wenches continued to sing tales of romantic weal and woe well into the seventeenth century can be ably attested by two references from the same year, 1653, the former from Issac Walton, the latter from Dorothy Osborne:

As I left this place and entered into the next field, a second pleasure entertained me; it was a handsome milkmaid, who cast away all care and sung like a nightingale; her voice was good, and the ditty fitted for it; it was that smooth song made by Kit Marlow, now at least fifty years ago; and the milkmaid's mother sung an answer to it, which was made by Sir Walter Raleigh in his younger days.[8]

The heat of the day is spent in reading or working, and about six or seven o'clock I walk out into a common that lies hard by the house, where a great many young wenches keep sheep and cows, and sit in the

139

shade singing of ballads.[9]

Young wenches sharing ballads in the shade certainly qualifies as a communal process. As regards our ballad though, evidence of a once-communal process seems initially thin (even on transplanted ground). In this it is not alone. An inevitable corollary of transition from communal performance to individual recital has been the deletion of communal elements not integral to a song's internal sense. In the case of ballads like 'The Fair Flower of Northumberland', where the refrain intervened in lines two and four of each verse, the deletion of the refrain would have rendered the song nonsensical, hence its preservation.

In the case of 'The Dæmon Lover', though its six British guises have failed to yield a single refrain, a couple of dozen American renditions favour a proximate, a repeated-last line that makes for a five-line verse (or even a repeated-last couplet, making for a six-line verse). In a mere five instances, the five-line verse also repeats the final word (or syllable) the first time it is sung, thus:

> For fear there may be strife, strife,
> For fear there may be strife.

Two of these five renditions - containing repeated word *and* line - are key representatives of unsullied British tradition, t'wit the version by Miss Tyrah Lam collected by Wilkinson in 1935 (see chapter two), and the one collected from Mrs Ellen Sullivan by Helen Flanders in 1932 (see chapter three) - that is, the famous 'George Allis' variant. The chances of these two variants both acquiring a latterday refrain from American tradition, whilst preserving their virgin-like state textually, are a tad remote. The most likely prognosis remains, once again, a more faithful retention of a British original - i.e. a refrain in its communal phase that fell by the quayside as it entered a less interactive domain.

During its communal phase, though, it would have enjoyed a quite different form of transmission from the travelling minstrel, whose day had already passed by 1589 if Puttenham's account, in his treatise *The Art Of English Poesie*, is to be taken at face value:

Popular musickes, [sung] by these Cantabanqui upon benches and

barrel-heads, where they have none other audience than boys or countrey fellowes that passe by them in the streete, or else by blind harpers or such like tavern minstrels, that give a fit of mirth for a groat, and their matters being for the most part stories of old time, as the tale of Sir Topas, the reports of Bevis of Southampton, Guy of Warwicke, Adam Bell, and Clymme of the Clough, and other such old romances or historical rhymes, *made purposely for recreation of the common people* [my italics] at Christmas dinners and brideales, and in taverns and alehouses, and such other places of base resort.[10]

The poignancy of the scene Puttenham is describing, evidently lost on him, should not be lost on us. Puttenham is describing the merest afterglow of an all-but-dead tradition. That the travelling minstrels, once a most honoured caste had, by 1589, been reduced to giving "a fit [a set number of verses] of mirth for a groat" suggests popular minstrelsy was reaching the end of its span of days. "Historical rhymes" like 'Adam Bell' were rarely 'sung' (in the sense now understood), and faded from oral tradition with the minstrel. None of the 'rhymes' cited here or in *The Complaynt*, 'Tam Lin' excepted, resembled the romantic ballads now sung by "knitters in the sun."

Though the knitters, milkmaids, shepherds and yeomen of the sixteenth century must have had a common store of ballads and lyrics, the overlap might not have been as great as scholars have perhaps imagined. The themes reverberating through 'The Dæmon Lover' suggest a song whose main appeal would have been to womenfolk. Would a ballad of such supernatural vngeance, which places the focus so roundly upon the woman and her broken vows, suggest composition by a well-versed sixteenth century yeoman (I say compose rather than write to neatly sidestep the contentious issue of whether such ballads were orally composed. I think not, but it does not fundamentally affect my argument)? Would such a song have been adopted by the travelling minstrel? 'The Dæmon Lover' certainly does not come across as a tavern song. On the other hand, the appeal to superstitious "knitters in the sun" dreaming of an escape from the drudgery of daily existence seems self-evident. Indeed American folklorist Alan Lomax, in his *Folk Songs of North America*, saw this as the key to its enduring appeal in the backwoods of America:

This song was sung by women who had come with their men to Pennsylvannia and the lowlands - by their daughters who lived and died hard in mountain log cabins - in turn, by their daughters sinking deeper in the squalor of backwoods life. For them, the easiest path out of a bad marriage was to run off with another man. Yet that way, the road of adventure, they would lose what they had and die in guilt, far from their children ... No fantasy could have been better calculated to reinforce the Calvinist sexual morality of our ancestors.[11]

And some kind of a distinction between 'men ballads' and 'women ballads' *has* been posited by a few commentators. Johannes Steenstrup, in his groundbreaking study of *The Medieval Popular Ballad* (1891), made women almost the sole recorders of tradition:

I entertain no doubt that if we succeeded in gaining a knowledge of the genuine popular poetry of the Catholic Middle Ages, we should have to render our thanks exclusively to the noble ladies of the sixteenth and seventeenth centuries.[12]

Unfortunately Steenstrup was writing in Danish, of Danish popular ballads, and his views have had little impact on Anglo-American studies, where the notion that this might be a perennial facet of popular tradition has never taken hold.

Just such a notion, though, was expressed by the English eccentric, Alfred Williams, who, shortly after the First World War, began scouting the environs of the upper Thames valley ("that part between Oxford, Abingdon and Wantage on the one hand, and Swindon, Purton and Cirencester on the other"[13]) in search of traditional ballads and songs. Undertaking this work without reference to any field-collectors of the English Folk Song Society then active, Williams remained seemingly unaware of any major scholastic work on the subject. As such, his theories were refreshingly free of the intellectual baggage of the literati, being drawn solely from his own personal experiences collecting from the country folk of southern England:

The women's songs were chiefly the sweetest of all. This is as befits the feminine nature. They were rarely sung by the males. The women might sing some of the men's pieces, but the men seldom sang those of the women. They appreciated their sweetness but they felt that the songs did not belong to them. There can be no doubt but that many choice and rare old songs, comparatively unknown, existed in the memories of the cottage dames. They are obviously more difficult to obtain than are those of the males. Most of the men sang at the inns, and their pieces were consequently more or less publicly known, while the women's songs were sung over the cradle and might not often have been heard out of doors. I have never omitted an opportunity of searching for the women's songs, where I suspected any to exist, and I was never disappointed with anything I obtained as the result of such inquiries. Examples of the kind and quality of songs sung by women are discovered in such pieces as 'Lord Thomas and Fair Eleanor' ... 'Lord Lovel' ... 'Cold blows the Winter's Wind' and so on.[14]

One of the striking aspects of the vast body of ballads and songs collected from Scottish tradition is just how beholden we are to female repositories of that tradition (this is to some extent parallelled in England and America, though collecting methodology may have distorted the true picture). It frequently appears as if the baton passed from generation to generation through some defined matriarchal line. Though a son or husband may have drawn from that tradition (how many instances are there in Bronson of a man singing a ballad "learnt from his mother"?), popular balladry - at least the form of balladry defined by the romantic and the supernatural - seems to have been transmitted this way from 'way back when'.

Sadly, not all the important nineteenth century Scottish collectors of oral tradition were willing to document their sources. Buchan failed, in mss. or publications, to cite sources, as did Herd, making our two best sources of Scottish traditional ballad texts, our worst sources of information. However, though Buchan's two 'best' sources were both men, James Rankin and James Nicol, neither is likely to have been the source for 'James Herries'. Nicol can be discounted, while Buchan did not first encounter Rankin until January 1827 when he had all but completed Ancient Ballads And Songs, the volume in which 'James Herries' appears.

In correspondence with Motherwell in January 1826, Buchan admits, "there are yet a few old women in this part of the country that I intend to wait upon, as I am informed they possess some rare and curious old [ballads]."[15] As his search progressed he refers at various points to valuable correspondents like "a young lady who resides with an aged lady, aged 80 years, and who has already sent me many scarce and curious pieces of antiquity,"[16] and, most memorably, in a letter dated 31 July, 1826:

> **I have been traversing the country of late in search of all the old syrens in 'hill, and holt, and moor and fen,' and have found several from whose decayed and time-worn memories, and by means of a bribe or fair promise, I have been enabled(sic) to extract several sweet morsels. An old woman of eighty got so much into the spirit of the olden time, that, on my approach, although lying on a bed by the fire, and whose decayed body and limbs could not carry her to the door, sat up and repeated many fragments which I had never heard before.[17]**

Scott often alluded to his sources in annoying generalities - "from tradition, with some conjectural emendations" - though his *Scotch Ballads, Material for Border Minstrelsy*, housed at Abbotsford, frequently takes us back to his sources. Only a minority of items in the *Minstrelsy* were derived by Scott himself from reciters, though he did take down a few ballad texts from Mrs Hogg, the mother of his friend James Hogg, who, upon being shown one of Scott's transcriptions, delivered the ultimate putdown of his endeavours:

> **They were made for singing and no for reading, but ye hae broken the charm now and they'll never be sung mair. And the warst thing o' a', they're nouther right spell'd, nor right setten down.[18]**

Though Kinloch and Motherwell came of a more fastidious generation of collectors, in Kinloch's case we are still reliant upon acknowledgments in his published collection and passing references in his ms. for information as to who provided the bulk of his texts. However, those who did warrant a Kinloch name-check were exclusively women: Miss Elizabeth Beattie, her sister Catherine, Jenny Watson, Mrs. Comie of Abderdeen, Mrs Charles of Torry and even Kinloch's niece, Miss M. Kinnear, whom he credits with 'The Elfin Knight' and 'The Laird of Lochnie'. Kinloch's most impressive source was a Mary Barr of Lesmahago, who provided around a third of the 46 items that comprise the first volume of his ms.

144

Motherwell did usually cite sources in his manuscript (now housed at Harvard), and Child, in appropriating the items for *English & Scottish Popular Ballads*, included this information. However, Motherwell also kept a notebook (at least for the years 1826-27) detailing his ballad-hunting exercises, which provides a list of fourteen "old singing women" in Renfrewshire, nine of whom he had already tracked down, plus five more that he hoped to. It includes the reported repertoires of some of these "old singing women." Thus a Miss Brown of Glasgow, who "learned a number of ballads from her blind Aunt, Nanny Brown," could sing 'The Golden Vanity', 'Geordie', 'Gil Morice', 'Jamie Douglas', 'Johnie Faa', 'Young Tamlin', 'Andrew Lammie', 'Young Beichan', 'Johnnie Armstrong', and 'Robin Hood and the Pedlar', all save the last two being of a romantic cast. Widow McCormick, from Paisley, "while dwelling in Dumbarton about 30 years there learned from an old woman in that place," the likes of 'Child Norice', 'Sweet William's Ghost', 'Tam Lin', 'The Knight and Shepherd's Daughter', 'The Brown Girl' and 'May Coleen'[19], ballads that happily straddle the supernatural and the romantic.

But the most famous of all the "singing women" who unlocked Scottish balladry for the literary antiquarians was undoubtedly Mrs Brown of Falkland, who gave Scott and Jamieson some of their very best texts, including the likes of 'Sir Hugh', 'Rose the Red and White Lily', 'The Gay Goshawk', 'Fair Annie', 'Childe Waters', 'The Lass of Rock Royal', 'Willie's Lady', 'Gil Brenton', 'Thomas the Rhymer', 'Bonny Bee Hom' and 'Clerk Colvill'. Mrs. Brown did not contribute a single 'border ballad' or Robin Hood ballad. Bronson considered her ballads, exemplified by the above, indicative of a personal bias on Mrs. Brown's part:

> There are occasional moral observations and pious reflections, especially at the end of her ballads, which are little above the broadside level and which jar our sense of fitness. It can hardly be an accident that where the erotic note is bluntly struck in other versions, in Mrs. Brown's it is side-stepped or soft-pedaled ... She pitches for the most part upon the marvellous, the supernatural, and the sentimentally romantic; and in her appetite for the last she is avid to the point of wholly uncritical acceptance of the most insipid folly. All these factors help to define the refracting influences always at work upon a body of traditional song, even in the presence of a first-class transmitting instrument.[20]

In fact, Mrs Brown's preference for "the marvellous, the supernatural, and the sentimentally romantic" might well be the defining trait of female Scottish ballad-singers. David Buchan considers Mrs. Brown's repertoire "very definitely ... a woman's corpus, and may [even] represent a woman's tradition within the regional tradition."[21] Such a tradition is to a large extent shared by the two great female ballad repositories of the early twentieth century: Bell Robertson, Gavin Greig's most remarkable find, who received her education from a wizened old spinster who lived by singing, and gave Greig over forty Child ballads including the likes of 'The Elphin Knight', 'Lady Isabel and the Elf-Knight', 'The Cruel Mother', 'Tam Lin' and 'The Twa Musicians'; and Bell Duncan, an equally remarkable find by the American James Carpenter, whose contribution to twentieth century Scottish tradition remains all but unknown because of Carpenter's failure to publish any of his findings from three years of determined collecting in the British Isles (an oversight apparently about to be corrected by the English *Folk Music Journal*).

Perhaps two of the last links in a chain of tradition, Bell Robertson and Bell Duncan would have remained anonymous librarians to a lost past had not Greig and Carpenter requested the right to browse through their store of traditional songs and ballads. Carpenter himself, describing his fortuitous discovery of Bell Duncan, caught a glimpse of that matriarchal line through tradition that even in the late 1920s remained surprisingly intact:

> If you're working a place: when you find one folk singer, he's likely to know two or three others ... [the first one] directed me to Bell Duncan, he thought she'd know some ballads. I went and knocked at the door, and finally an elderly woman with a fine forehead, great big forehead and keen, clear eyes, with a beautiful shawl on her shoulder, came to the door. I told her who I was, and she looked me up and down and turned straight around to her turnips that she was cooking on the crane over the peat fire. Her daughter came downstairs and heard me talking, and I told her that Mr. Campbell had sent me. She called her mother round, and I said I wondered whether [she] knew any ballads. She said, "Well, I might. I might know some." And so the next day I came around with my typewriter and started copying down some titles ... and before I knew it, I had three or four pages full of titles. And I thought to myself, "Well, this woman is certainly

crazy." ... [but] all summer long I was copying her ballads - 300 songs and ballads, amounting to 400 seven-stanza pages. And she never gave me a version without the tune with it.[22]

(xii) The golden age of Pop Balladry?

Though at first the bard combines both trades, music and poetry, after a time poetry and music begin to specialize on their own. We can see the turning-point in the magnificent lutanist songbooks published between 1590 and 1643 (the exact period which saw the differentiation of the Blank Verse drama from the old interludes and morality plays) where the lute gradually takes the greater share of the partnership to itself: with few exceptions the words of the songs verge on the trivial, yet seldom are quite worthless. They are still performing a useful part, but they suggest the faithful friend of the hero in a novel or epic, a foil to greatness. - Robert Graves.[1]

The singers that the likes of Buchan, Kinloch, Motherwell and the Scotts encountered do not appear to have felt it beholden to them to compose, or consciously adulterate, the ballads they sung. And yet the ballads they collected had clearly evolved, sustaining separate identities, before the collectors came to claim them. 'The Dæmon Lover' acquired at least two, and possibly three, Scottish templates prior to its dispersal, all of which were clearly conscious reworkings and none of which could have been the result of some quasi-spontaneous utilization of balladic formulae.

Herein lies an essential contradiction: how could a tradition that lurched from a form of stasis to debilitation have devolved from one that was truly alive? Could it really be that these narrative songs, sung by country-folk, did not originate with the same folk's ancestors but were somehow adopted and preserved by the folk as best they could? What Bertrand Bronson has entitled "the coefficient of [consistent and productive] change"[2] resolves the contradiction and provides for the sort of conditions likely to instigate the popular ballad form, i.e. that chink in time when popular narrative songs composed for the people became popular narrative songs composed for *and* by the people. It is this change that signalled the genuine birth of popular song.

The reworking of minstrel ballads may have been one way of preserving their popular appeal but the ballads that survived from the fifteenth and sixteenth centuries, to be collected in the nineteenth, were very much

'The Greatest Hits of the Golden Age of Balladry'. As we have seen, even as remarkable a ballad as 'The Dæmon Lover' was passing from der volk charts by the end of the eighteenth century, for even in a folk tradition that respects and preserves the past, most ballads - and most ballad templates - must have lived and died within a narrow geographic band, over a relatively short period of time. A statistical comparison of Child ballads collected from Scottish tradition in the early nineteenth and twentieth centuries suggests that something like 77 Child ballads had dropped from tradition in the intervening years, close to half of those collected between 1765 and 1830.

Whilst many derivatives would have died some way upstream, some Child ballads have undoubtedly come down to us without their 'lost' original. Hence the problems for those who have sought to draw a direct line between the minstrel ballad, or indeed the broadside, and its popular derivative. George Lyman Kittredge has asserted that, "the popular ballads are really popular [because] they belong to the folk,"[3] but the folk are, and always have been, an amorphous lot. As long as the balladeer and the audience remained chained to the same frame, then the forces of conservation and innovation operated like a well-oiled see-saw. Making some ballads anew, preserving the perennials and dispensing with the anachronistic was the popular balladeer's role from the onset of the sixteenth to the early years of the eighteenth centuries, when the audience-balladeer contract seems to have been severed by Reason. Bertrand Bronson acknowledged this:

> The coefficient of change - speaking now particularly of consistent and not disruptive change - [is reflected in] the level of intelligence of the folk-singing community, and the liveliness of its artistic sensibility. The higher that level, the more unwilling - indeed, unable - a singer will be to serve merely as a passive transmitter of the songs that he has loved. Those students who have maintained that there was, hundreds of years ago, a creative period of oral tradition, but that since the sixteenth century or thereabouts tradition in balladry has been on the road downhill, have really been saying the same thing. ... Faced on the one hand with a number of superior early ballad texts, and on the other by the spectacle of increasing dilapidation in the multiplying evidence of the variants collected from recent tradition, their conclusion was in fact almost the only rational one possible. The spread of literacy has drawn off into other channels a

large proportion of the creative energy which once went into ballads.[4]

It was in such an enviroment - when "the level of intelligence of the folk-singing community" was at its historical peak - that 'The Dæmon Lover' came to be written, as the borders and northern marches witnessed a resplendent new artform - popular balladry. Bronson's quote above, though it mistakenly blames "the spread of literacy" for the shift in worldview, hints at a "golden age of balladry" in or around the sixteenth century.

In what sense did sixteenth century social conditions create a "coefficient of [consistent] change" that allowed popular balladry to draw strength, just as the minstrel ballad was drawing its last breath? As early as the middle of the century, the advent of the broadside press in London, Edinburgh and Oxford, and the decline of a minstrel class may have left only the most static section/s of the population in charge of a way of expressing themselves in honest song.

Perhaps even Bronson underestimated the "level of intelligence" of sixteenth century "knitters in the sun" and their ability to formulate ballads. Rather than sharing Child's view that these figures came at the end of the golden age of popular balladry, he believed that "there is ... reason to surmise that Scottish balladry was of comparatively late growth ... [and] that it reached its fullest development [not] much before the eighteenth century."[5] And yet, almost without exception, those ballads whose composition can be assuredly allocated to the late seventeenth and eighteenth century suggest little more than a compendium of platitudes and conventional formulae.

This need not undermine the central tenet of Bronson's proposition: that an oral process in which "passive transmitters of tradition" simply preserved an extant canon ought to be pushed some way forward, to a time when "a large proportion of the creative energy which once went into ballads ... [has been] drawn off into other channels," i.e. the late eighteenth century.

Unfortunately, we simply do not have any pre-eighteenth century Scottish texts with which to examine Bronson's plausible supposition that the 'oral process' is bound by the "level of intelligence of the folk community" (the editor of the Percy folio called on no Scottish sources and in so far as earlier versions of the folio ballads can be traced, they come from English sources). One is required to *assume* that even 'The Dæmon Lover' variants collected in the years 1803-1830 were some decades removed from that intelligent folk community. Certainly the versions collected post-Child argue against oral tradition *since 1769* ever being "as efficient a cause of the ballad in question as the original creative act of the individual author."[6]

And yet the evidence to support Bronson's proposition - positive change as a prerequisite of a buoyant ballad tradition - can still be found in the "ideological strata" underlying nineteenth and twentieth century traditional texts of 'The Dæmon Lover'. The 'cast his glamour o'er her' verse, the atmospheric if incongruous 'cloven foot thrusting through', even possibly that harrowing final verse, smack of later interpolations, albeit ones that cut their swathe through tradition before the end of the seventeenth century. The supposition at the end of this particular tunnel asserts that the original 'dæmonic' text - an amalgam of Scott and Motherwell E - and a Buchanite rewrite - probably incorporating verses 2 and 11 of the Glenbuchat text - were both extant by the end of the sixteenth century, both being indicative of "a [highly] creative period of oral tradition."[7] Though the Buchanite text, by forming a prototype for a 1657 English broadside, acquired a specific historic lock, the 'dæmonic' text was surely the 'original' - hence the seven year "span of days," the allusion to 'Thomas the Rhymer', and the dæmon lover's preternatural powers.

If Bronson's Proposition is allowed to hold the floor, then throughout the sixteenth and seventeenth centuries the would-be traditional balladeer would have been as likely as our friend Laurence Price to rework a popular ballad, sometimes to such an extent that it became something altogether different. 'Fause Knight On The Road', 'Erlinton', 'Henry Martyn' and 'Captain Wedderburn's Courtship' are all examples of Child ballads 'derived' from other Child ballads - 'The Elphin Knight', 'Earl Brand', 'Sir Andrew Barton' and 'A Riddle Wisely Expounded' respectively. Such reworkings were presumably only rarely adopted:

the mere question: What constitutes identity in ballads? is, in truth, a philosophical - a metaphysical - question, to which Child kept

151

making practical, unmetaphysical answers. We need look no further than the variants of Child's no.1 - 'Riddles Wisely Expounded' - to realize that undemonstrable assumptions must be nine-tenths of any definition of A Ballad in the group sense of the term ... Why do we call Child no.1A*, of ca. 1450, and Motherwell's narrativeless 1D and Mrs. Texas Gladden's Virginia copy in the Library of Congress phonograph archive the *same* ballad?[8]

Likewise, can we consider Buchan[243C], Scott [243F] and the two 'House Carpenter' texts collected by Helen Flanders [Sullivan & Price] the 'same ballad'? Two quite distinct Scottish sensibilities composed the different templates of 'The Dæmon Lover' - dæmonic and revenant, both adopted by tradition - the latter forming the basis for a rationalized English derivative, the former retaining its dæmonic aspect without ever making the journey south.

Whether a *3rd* Scottish variant, the Motherwell-Price text, which independently span off from our dæmon original, was an early reworking I doubt we'll ever know. That it complies with all the criteria of "creative tradition" - welding together, as David Buchan wrote in his thoughtful 1972 study, *The Ballad & The Folk,* all the "dramatic, lyric, and narrative elements...into a perfectly unified whole"[9] - need not be in doubt.

Dr. Buchan argued that the bulk of Scottish ballads in Child's collection were collected during what he terms the 'transitional period' "from a condition of nonliteracy to a condition of literacy"[10], which he dated to the seventy years that separate the sources for Mrs. Brown's ballads (c.1759) from Buchan's (c.1828). Though I suspect David Buchan, in his self-imposed oral-formulaic straitjacket, dramatically overstated the importance of a new literacy, he did recognize and highlight an irreversible sea-change in popular balladry at the end of the eighteenth century brought on by economic and societal forces:

> The aesthetic hallmark of the oral ballad is that it welds together into a perfectly unified whole dramatic, lyric, and narrative elements. In telling his story the maker concerns himself with what the characters do, how the characters feel, and how the characters interact with one another. He varies his scenes of narrative action, of emotional release and of

dramatic confrontation to achieve a smooth blending of tones in the complete ballad. As the irreducible core of a ballad-story is the interaction of a few characters, we may say that the dramatic element is the predominating one and that it subsumes the narrative and lyrical elements. In the transitional texts, this is no longer the case. They manifest a distinct lack of subtlety in the tonal variation from scene to scene ... The binding dramatic element decreases in force and effect, and the narrative and emotional elements assume a greater prominence. Many versions begin dramatically and forcefully, then tail off because the singer thereafter concentrates on telling the story in flat sequential narrative, or concentrates on the emotions aroused by one event within the entire story.[11]

A "concentrat[ion] on the emotions aroused by one event within the entire story" certainly provides the neatest of summaries of the naturalized texts of 'The House Carpenter' encountered in twentieth-century America. "Oral tradition" in early twentieth century America has been a long way removed from the kind of creative oral tradition that spawned the popular ballad form. The American texts, some splendid as renditions (see discography), stand as a pretty miserable bunch on the page. Which is not to suggest that the process by which "a three dimensional view of the ballad" was "succeeded by a two-dimensional view" did not impact as widely, or as quickly, in the British Isles. David Buchan, recognized "the [same] disintegration of the oral patternings"[12] in latterday Northeast Scottish texts.

Some American renditions of Child ballads may have suffered unduly from geographic and social dislocation and the same ballads - as collected by Greig, Duncan, Ord and Carpenter in Scotland c.1900-30 - may benefit from more rounded narratives but even here "the binding dramatic element" had clearly been in free-fall for a century or more, with 'motivational' and emotional elements assuming a far greater role.

Though we have no usable post-transitional Scottish text of 'The Dæmon Lover' to assert the same disintegration, we do have a complete English rendition transcribed as recently as 1889, a century and a half after the song's publication in *A Collection Of Diverting Songs*. Collected by Sabine Baring-Gould in Holcome Burnell, it corresponds almost word for word with the *Diverting Songs* broadside for its first eight verses (equivalent to the printed verses 1-6 and 8-9) and its final two. The remaining nine verses expand verses nine to twelve in *A Collection Of Diverting Songs* to more than twice their 'original' length, taking the 'lingering' technique deployed by most traditional balladeers to an almost parodic level:

> 9. They had not rowed a bowshot off,
> A bowshot on the main,
> But o'er her shoulder she looked back,
> "I would I were home again."

> 10. They had not rowed a bowshot off,
> A bowshot on the main,
> But o'er her shoulder she looked and said,
> Set me back on the yellow sand!

> 11. For I have a child in my little chamber
> And I think I hear him cry
> I would not, I would not, my babe should wake
> And his mother not standing by.

> 12. The Captain he smiled and stroked his arms
> And said, This may not be
> Behind is the shore and the sea is before
> And thou must go, sweet love, with me.

> 13. She had not been long upon the sea
> Not long upon the deep,
> Before that she was wringing her hands,
> And loudly did wail and weep.

> 14. O why do you wail, and wherefore weep?
> And wring your hands? said he,
> Do you weep for the gold that lies in the hold
> Or do you weep for my fee?

> 15. I do not weep for your gold, she said;
> Nor do I weep for your fee,
> But by the mast-head is my baby dead,

And I weep for my dead baby.

16. She had not abeen upon the seas,
The days they were three or four,
And never a word she spoke, nor stirred
And she looked towards the shore.

17. She had not abeen upon the seas,
But six days of the week,
Before that she lay as cold as the clay
And never a word could speak.

18. They had not sailed upon the seas,
Of weeks but three and four,
But down to the bottom the ship did swim,
And never was heard of more.[13]

Baring-Gould's rendition is as resolutely rational as the eighteenth century broadside (save for the surreal line "by the masthead/ is my baby dead," which I do not pretend to comprehend). The 'lingering' trio of verses that precedes the sinking of the ship, with its little calendar of days - "The days they were three or four", "But six days of the week", "Of weeks but three and four," - lacks the drama of Scottish renditions but retains the whiff of tradition. Verses nine and ten, with their descriptive "bowshot off the main", could well be floating verses that have attached themselves to this ballad somewhere down the pike.

However, three of the seven 'new' verses also contain internal rhymes in the third line. Though these occur in many a seventeenth- and eighteenth-century broadside (the Robin Hood broadsides in Child's collection have an unhealthy smattering of such hackneyed internal rhymes, a stylistic throwback to the days of minstrelsy), they are also clumsy enough in execution to suggest the work of a latter-day poetaster:

> *Behind is the shore/ and the sea is before. (v.9)*
> *But by the mast-head/ is my baby dead, (v.11)*
> *Before that she lay/ as cold as the clay, (v.15)*

John Burrison, in a recent article, has in fact suggested that the Baring-Gould text is "a truly creative [sic] reworking of the [eighteenth century] broadside by a gifted folk poet ... [probably] an Anglicized Irishman or someone closely acquainted with Anglo-Irish folksong, because of the apparent fondness for internal rhyme. He must have approved of the broadside's beginning and end for he kept them intact."[14] That the song was reworked from within tradition (rather than from the printed page) seems bourne out by the tune Baring-Gould collected, which is of the same genus as one known by the Christie family of Banffshire earlier in the century (see appendix of tunes).

When it comes to the dubious virtues of 'transitional' and post-'transitional' "secondary act[s] of composition," it took Gerould to note that metaphysical moonshine at work again:

> **I must confess that I feel a touch of eighteenth-century Teutonic mysticism still hanging about the emphasis laid in these theories upon the importance of oral transmission. It has of course been a *vera causa* in bringing about the condition in which most ballads have reached us, and one need not quarrel with the statement of Menendez Pidal that at any moment of the process beauty may drop in. It is, however, also true that it has [most] often worked for degeneration.[15]**

It is high time scholars poured some of that 'metaphysical moonshine' down the sink and recognized that the authors of the great popular ballads count for something, anonymous as they may be, and that the oral process should not be the primary focus of ballad studies but a conduit back to a time when "the level of intelligence of the folk community" was such that ballads like 'The Dæmon Lover' were created and renewed from within a common, vibrant tradition.

The available evidence suggests that post-'transitional' oral tradition has rarely encouraged "the process [of] beauty," however valuable a resource the many variants collected in the twentieth century may be, and however much they "may contribute much toward the solution of some of the problems that now vex the student of popular traditions."[16]

The "weigh[ing], sift[ing], and select[ing]" of components that "most accurately express the popular taste and the popular ideal"[17] in America has, in the case of 'The Dæmon Lover' (and, indeed, other supernatural ballads like 'Love Henry', 'A Riddle Wisely Expounded' &c.), resulted in a threadbare "domestic" ballad, to appropriate A.L. Lloyd's phrase, from a ballad with truly mythic sweep; has stripped the revenant first of his motive, and then his identity, making the (inevitable) act of retribution a simple twist of fate (the ship sinks).

If the latterday American texts of 'The House Carpenter' are examples of community selection then the American folk process has been largely deleterious, at least where British ballads are concerned. Perhaps this is not too surprising. Removing a popular ballad from its wellspring is bound to result in an identity crisis, which may be resolved by naturalizing the ballad in question ('Pretty Peggy-O'), but is more likely simply to create a series of incongruities that certain academics may embrace as the mark of Americana, but is really the insignia of lost connections.

Given the unlikelihood of the "level of intelligence of the [modern] folk community" equalling that of the golden age of Scottish balladry, the result must be deterioration or, at best, stasis. The "popular ideal" of which Cecil Sharp writes in *English Folk Song: Some Conclusions* is precisely that, a chimera on some metaphysical horizon. The sooner it stops defining 'the oral process', the better our chances of understanding the essential relationship between Mystery and creativity in the folk tradition:

> **Rationalization is one of the most powerful of all the forces that work on ballads. In Britain and America as belief in ghosts, fairies, and other spiritual characters dwindles, everyday substitutes are provided, so that an elfin knight becomes a gypsy lover and later an illicit lover or even the lodger, while a mermaid is replaced by a mortal, if mysterious, sweetheart. So strong is such rationalization that most of our modern versions of the old ghost, witch &c. ballads have lost all or nearly all traces of the supernatural. Thus 'James Harris' generally appears today as a triangle love tale between three mortals, the harp motif has nearly vanished from 'The Twa Sisters', and Sir Hugh's body seldom speaks miraculously from the well.[18]**

And yet 'The Twa Sisters', 'Sir Hugh' and 'James Harris' remain three of the most enduring Child ballads in American tradition ('The Twa Sisters' provides a particularly interesting case study because the 'supernatural' denouement - the hair of the murdered sister being used to string a minstrel's harp, which then accuses the surviving sibling of her murder - detached itself at some point, assuming a separate identity as 'The Wind and the Rain'). Given that 'Sir Hugh' has thus become simply a particularly nasty murder ballad and a libel upon Jews, and 'The House Carpenter' a curious tale of infidelity and a libel on sailors, one might have expected both songs to vanish from tradition. Not so.

But since 'The Dæmon Lover' had already become rationalized by the time it began making Atlantic crossings, save for a rogue strain, why did the ballad not only survive, but flower in the New World, when its olde worlde charm failed to preserve it in the motherland? After all, omitting the final act in this four-act playlet, and prefering an anti-climactic epilogue to the actual circumstances of the lady's punishment, surely subverts the original didactic nature of the tale. Could it be that the mundanity of the American song still hides "ideological strata ... from all the savage and heroic ages,"[19] as A.L. Lloyd has suggested?

Carl Sandburg implied, in his introduction to 'House Carpenter' in *American Songbag*, that it has been the quaintness of the tale that has encouraged retention in tradition:

> **This is among the hoary and tarnished keepsakes of the ballad world ... The House Carpenter in style, story, method, has some of the leading characteristics of many of the oldest ballads ... [and] is as quaint to some of us as a mezzotint portrait in the lid of a snuff box of one of General Washington's staff officers.**[20]

Alan Lomax, in his own introduction to the song in *Folk Songs Of North America*, recognized that the ballad acquired a new moral stain once it came to America - in true broadside fashion, it had once again become a warning to married women:

> **The present ballad, one of the favourite folk songs of early America, but an especial favourite in the South, characterizes man as a tempting demon and romantic love as a temptation that destroys women. In the British original the returned lover, James Harris, is actually a**

demon from Hell (in some versions the Devil himself) ... The Devil
disappeared from most American versions, but the man stands out, as all
the more demonic, as Death himself. The woman, believing her first lover is
dead, marries and has a secure home with children. The old lover returns
and offers her an escape. In the first moments of her romantic adventure,
she is splendid - "she glittered and glistened and proudly she walked" - till
she is "taken to be some queen." But this escape from domestic sordidness
lasts scarcely a month. She begins to weep - not for her house or her
husband, whom she despises, but for her children. Then, as a punishment
for her guilt, she and her lover sink in the sea to rise no more.[21]

Interestingly, Lomax makes the interpolated verse from 'Lord Thomas &
Fair Eleanor' the key to his interpretation. The notion that the sinking of
the ship is "a punishment for her guilt" is only implicit (at best) in the
nine-verse runt of a version Lomax published, collected first-hand in
1941. Only American texts that have preserved the dialogue regarding
'the hills of heaven and hell' suggest that she is indeed being judged and
punished, even if we are not sure why (pique?), and these represent
less than one in eight of the versions collected from American oral
tradition this century.

The reverence of *der volk* for British supernatural ballads perhaps stems
from an underlying subtext that might almost qualify as some kind of
racial memory, waiting to be brought out by the performance of such a
ballad. Greil Marcus stands on the brink when he writes, in 1997, of
Dock Bogg's 1927 version of 'Pretty Polly' (a derivative of 'Lady Isabel
and the Elphin Knight'):

> There is a supernatural tinge to the song as it emerges from Bogg's
> performance, even though nothing unearthly is named or even hinted at;
> the sulforous odour comes up because *as Boggs tells it* [my italics] there
> seems to be no will in the story, only fate, or ritual.[22]

Except that this 'supernatural tinge' does not require the specific tone
Boggs brings. It is found as easily in recordings of the same song by B.F.
Shelton, The Stanley Brothers, Jack Wallin or Dylan himself. Nor is this
sense of mystery American in origin, as Marcus seems to imply. Drawing
from a deep well of British tradition, its references come from "a
mythology once quite coherent but [that has] become fragmentary

through the passage of time."[23] David Buchan called it 'contextual force':

> **Through generations of use traditional language accrues a
> contextual force; it acquires connotative reverberations unrecognized by
> the ear untuned to tradition ... Ballads lack the similes and imagery of
> written literature, but what they do have ... is a kind of symbolic imagery.[24]**

The "mezzotint portrait in the lid of a snuff box" feel of a ballad like 'The
House Carpenter' comes from an unshakeable feeling that something
other than the words is going on in the song, that even waters as
seemingly shallow as the De Marsan 'House Carpenter' might have
once run deep. Dylan speared exactly the right metaphor when he
spoke of this kind of music as providing "the only true, valid death you
can feel today." In the subtexts of a phrase like "I have returned from the
salt, salt sea/ and all for the sake of thee," (the 'sake' not the 'love' - a
double-sided phrase, unfinished business, but not in the way she may
think) the 'real' identity of 'The Dæmon Lover' may still be found.
Revealing the identity of the ghost to the listener at the outset, as Dylan
does, heightens "the dramatic element," reclaiming a whole other level
of 'mystery' for the song.

Sadly, once the significance of the dæmon lover's promise to show her
the banks of Italy and the 'hills of heaven and hell' have passed from the
song, the story can only be secondary to the moral (or, as one
commentator recently put it, "American singers are less interested in the
sensational than in the moral issue and the fate and feelings of the
characters"[25]), and the traditional ballad - that form which, Graves
insists, "does not moralize or preach" - ceases to bury itself in mystery,
becoming no more valid a way to feel death than your average country
& western song.

(xiii) Me and the Devil.

A society which thinks, as ours thinks, that it has outlived the need for magic, is either mistaken in that opinion, or else it is a dying society, perishing for lack of interest in its own maintenance. - R.G. Collinwood.[1]

Much print has been expended, largely by American ballad-scholars, regarding the forces of rationalization in America that have ironed out many an interesting chink of tradition. With 'The House Carpenter', though, the processes of rationalization began to take effect some time before the song passed over the ocean. From the residual turns of phrase underlying some very ordinary American texts it is clear that both Scottish *and* English texts - or perhaps supernatural and 'natural' British texts - made it across the pond. If the power of English print seems to have won through in the end, there seem to have always been popular forces seeking to rationalize the story, to 'expand its constituency'.

That none of the traditional English or Manx texts have retained any supernatural elements does *not* allow us to presuppose an English supernatural text never existed, simply that conditions worked against its survival into the eighteenth century. The 1657 broadside of 'James Harris' confirms that the revenant nature of 'The Dæmon Lover' survived its original passage to England (I somehow doubt that Price collected the song in Scotland).

Not that even a relatively gentrified early Stuart yeoman would have had a great problem with the notion of a ghost returning to exact revenge for some wrong committed against their ex-person. Whilst some post-Reformation urbanite might have been made to feel uncomfortable by its diabolic element, "there are more things in heaven and earth than are dreamt of in [their] philosophy,"[2] as Hamlet first observed to the pragmatic Horatio circa 1602. Hamlet himself took great pains to ensure that what appeared to be the revenant spirit of his dead father was not some dæmonic sprite hoping to tempt him into murdering his 'innocent' uncle:

> The spirit that I have seen

161

May be the devil. And the devil hath power
T' assume a pleasing shape; yea, and perhaps
Out of my weakness and my melancholy,
As he is very potent with such spirits,
Abuses me to damn me.[3]

i.e. exactly what the Devil does in 'The Dæmon Lover': assuming a
"pleasing shape" to abuse and damn the carpenter's wife. In this sense,
the early broadside press, though it revelled in the fantastic and
delighted in the ludicrous, was still reliant upon a welcome credulity from
its readership, something Shakespeare himself lampooned in a famous
passage from 'The Winter's Tale':

MOPSA: I love a ballad in print o' life, for then we are sure they are true.
AUTOLYCUS: Here's a ballad of a fish that appeared upon the west on
Wednesday the fourscore of April, forty thousand fathom above water and sung
this ballad against the hard hearts of maids. It is thought she was a woman and
was turned into a cold fish for she would not exchange kisses with one that loved
her. The ballad is very pitiful and as true.[4]

The transition from the revenant 'James Harris' to the mortally-grieved
'Ship-Carpenter' is in many ways simply a barometer of societal change,
one that, though it did not bypass Scotland, impacted more slowly there.
The explicit having become implicit, became finally absent. From the
explicit 'James Harris' to the absent 'Distressed Ship-Carpenter' is a
mere eighty years but then by 1737 the Age of Reason, anathema to the
supernatural ballad, was upon the land. Hence the willingness of
Regency balladeers to satirize such ghostly tales, ridiculing traditional
forms (and those who drew solace from them), as George Colman did
famously in 'The Unfortunate Miss Bailey':

A Captain bold, in Halifax, who dwelt in country quarters,
Seduced a maid, who hang'd herself, one morning, in her garters,
His wicked conscience smited him, he lost his stomach daily,
He took to drinking rafatee, and thought upon Miss Bailey.

One night betimes he went to rest, for he had caught a fever,
Says he, "I am a handsome man, but I'm a gay deceiver."
His candle just at twelve o'clock began to burn quite paley,

A ghost stepp'd up to his bedside, and said, "Behold Miss Bailey!"

"Avaunt, Miss Bailey!" then he cried, "your face looks white and mealy,"
"Dear Captain Smith," the ghost replied, "you've used me ungenteely;
The Crowner's Quest goes hard with me, because I've acted frailly,
And Parson Biggs won't bury me, though I am dead Miss Bailey!"

"Dear Corpse," said he, "since you and I accounts must once for all close,
I've really got a one-pound note in my regimental small clothes;
'Twill bribe the sexton for your grave." - The ghost then vanish'd gaily,
Crying, "Bless you, wicked Captain Smith, remember poor Miss Bailey."[5]

The few versions of 'House Carpenter' collected in the twentieth century - Dylan's included - where the singer has felt compelled to explain that the central figure is a ghost (or dæmon) are indicative of a lost connection, explicating the song to give it *back* its sense because the audience no longer expects the supernatural to impinge upon the natural world. In 'The Dæmon Lover', the wife is being punished for something as solemn as the breaking of marriage vows - whether by the spirit of 'James Harris', or some diabolic doppelganger. The punishment, an eternity of damnation, may seem a tad strong for modern sensibilities, but reflects a moral certitude about to be supplanted with an ambivalent existentialism by 'Enlightened' writers.

Just as Hamlet operated according to an Elizabethan 'world picture' that incorporated a pagan belief in revenants into Christian notions of damnation and judgement - colouring his every action (or inaction, if semantics is your game) - so does the carpenter's wife betray the same worldview. Knowing she has broken her vows, she accedes to a former obligation (the promise of riches, an unnecessary touch, probably reflects a later hand). Though she is duly punished, it is not for her greed or her fickleness but for the breaking of a solemn vow. Only when common folk decided that breaking such vows should not warrant eternal damnation did the need for a rationalized 'Dæmon Lover' arise. Unfortunately, such a sea-change coincided with the death of "the coefficient of [consistent and productive] change"[6], i.e. the spirit that inspired the (re)creation, not the mere disemination, of traditional ballads. As A.L. Lloyd succinctly put it in his *Folk Song of England* (1967):

> **The road of the ballad runs from the magical to the heroic to the domestic. What was once a kind of narrative incantation becomes a complex tale in recitative form whose aim is to encourage and inspire, and finally the sung narrative becomes a romance with little more purpose than to divert and entertain ... Yet in many of our ballads, domestic as they seem on the surface, ideological strata are found from all the savage and heroic ages that the ballad-idea has travelled through. - A.L. Lloyd[7]**

Constructing a literary history of one particularly enduring popular ballad, 'The Dæmon Lover', I have sought to mine the "idealogical strata ... from all the savage and heroic ages that [this particular] ballad-idea has travelled through," to hint at the rich tapestry to be found within the supernatural ballad-tradition - happily applying that term to tales of fairies, elphin knights, dæmons, revenants, and witchcraft - drawing on pertinent elements from stories-in-song as diverse as 'Tam Lin', 'Thomas the Rhymer', 'Young Hunting', 'Riddles Wisely Expounded', 'The Devil's Courtship', 'Sweet William's Ghost', 'The Grey Cock' and 'The Elphin Knight'. A more in-depth study of these ballads, I do not doubt, could lead to the definitive account of the supernatural ballad, a remarkable literary genre that existed among both the literate and the semi-literate in Britain and much of continental Europe between the fifteenth and eighteenth centuries. Whether the impetus for such a general study exists in the current climate, I know not.

That the surreal symbolism originally imprinted on these ballads has been gradually subsumed 'neath the homespun philosophizing favoured by the white rural folk of the American plains - what Wilfred Mellers described as "evolutionary elements ... fostered at the expense of antique virtues"[8] - has not seemingly impaired their durability. 'Love Henry' and 'The Two Sisters', two songs of metampsychosis recorded by Dylan in naturalized guise, have been among the most popular remnants of British balladry in American rural tradition. And while a nineteen-year old Dylan may have sung a naturalized 'Two Sisters' he later used the idea of a dead sister's accusing tone ringing out from a harp strung with her hair in his own masterful ballad, 'Percy's Song', where - at song's end - "the only tune my guitar would play was 'Oh the Cruel Rain and the Wind'." That American folk tradition has not generated its own set of ballads of superstitious ritual perhaps explains why the 'revivalists' turned to the British ballads when in need of that 'supernatural tinge'. Even the likes of 'Pretty Polly' and 'The Cuckoo Is A Pretty Bird', singled out as repositories of the Mysterious by Dr. Marcus, have remained resolutely British in type, whoever may have been exercising their vocal chords upon them.

Which is not to suggest that there has never been a "coefficient of [productive] change" in American tradition, simply that, like the British tradition, it happened in a period when popular creative tradition was isolated from those who monitor sea-changes in popular culture. There is almost no documentation from the mid-to-late nineteenth century of the coalescing of Anglo-American folk tradition with a budding Afro-American blues form, though Marshall W. Stearns suggested the most likely course of interaction in his *Story Of Jazz* (1956):

> European folksong is a little more complicated harmonically and African tribal music is a little more complicated rhythmically ... When the Africans arrived in the New World the folk music that greeted him must have sounded familiar enough, except for a lack of rhythm. The blending has proceeded on many levels and in a variety of ways.[9]

If a new kind of vibrancy was introduced along with Afro-American rhythmic sense, it is not surprising that the "coefficient of [productive] change," where it has been found in the twentieth century, has tended to be blues-based. As Samuel Charters, with a certain prescience, observed back in 1963, in *The Poetry Of The Blues*:

> The language of American popular song has lost its freshness and its ability to convey even strong emotion. The English folk tradition which produced the broadside ballads and the rich profusion of love song and social commentary has dwindled to a repetitive and almost meaningless manipulation of phrases which no longer have even the artistic power of the sentimental Victorian love poetry from which they are derived [sic]. As the years pass the blues may become as moribund as popular song has become ... as the developing blues audience forces the singer into repetitions of his own attitudes ... but the blues still have a fine, raw vigor.[10]

An oft-ignored aspect of 'the blues' - at least as represented by the primitive country-blues artists of the first third of the twentieth century - is the commonality shared with those "knitters in the sun" to whom I have ascribed the supernatural ballad form. Disenfranchised, and with few other creative outlets available, adhering to a Christianity with its own touch of the pagan about it, utilizing a musical form simple to acquire and yet perpetually opaque, and with its own lyrical templates, floating verses and conventional opening addresses - any takers on "I woke up this morning" as the Afro-American equivalent of "As I roved out one fine May morn"? - the blues was also a form whose golden age coinicided with the death-knell of a white rural tradition.

The "supernatural tinge" found in the British ballads - one that seemingly bypassed American ballad forms - certainly seems to have managed to hop, skip and jump into "the devil's music."

That the connection between superstitious ritual and creative tradition need not be confined to the highlands of Albion is surely ably attested by that most revered of blues shaman guitarist-singers, Robert Johnson. Taking his cue from the likes of Skip James, Kokomo Arnold, Henry Thomas and Lonnie Johnson, Johnson crafted songs suggestive of someone to whom the devil was no mere bugaboo, but a daily presence. The most direct paean to the diabolic in the Johnson canon remains 'Me and the Devil Blues' when, much like 'The Dæmon Lover', the Devil comes to the singer's door to claim his rotten soul. However, in Johnson's case there is no mistaking his visitor's identity:

> Early this morning,
> When you knocked upon my door,
> Early this morning,
> Peetie knocked upon my door,
> And I said, Hello Satan,
> I believe it's time to go.[11]

If Johnson had met his untimely end a mere decade earlier, he would have had the same curse of anonymity reserved for him as the Scottish balladeers of the fifteenth and sixteenth centuries. That he was recorded at all was entirely fortuitous. Like many of his British predecessors his

166

was a purely aural education in the ways of sound and form, coming as he did during the last impasse between tradition and transition in popular song, the era of 'hillbilly' and 'race' 78s that ended with the Second World War.

Sadly, when the chain of tradition was broken, it was severed from within. Content to be singer-songwriters of a new *milieu*, the self-conscious solo artists that came after Dylan looked no further than the blues for the roots of popular song. As such perhaps only Dylan, among modern American singer-songwriters, has any real sense of first-hand contact with the last strands of the 'traditionalist' forms of Mystery, black and white. He said as much to Dave Marsh back into 1993, when dismissing the Marsh family's part-time paymaster, Bruce Springsteen, and his ilk: "They weren't there to see the end of the traditional people ... I was."[12]

However, in literary terms Dylan remains the greenhorn. The popular ballad has exercised a profound influence on some of the greatest poets of the last two centuries - Coleridge, Burns, Scott ("I overwhelmed my schoolfellows and all who would hearken to me with tragical recitations from the ballads of Bishop Percy['s *Reliques*]"[13]), Swinburne, Graves ("The ballads of 'Chevy Chase' and 'Sir Andrew Barton' ... were the first two real poems that I remember reading."[14]). Each has acknowledged his debt in verse and prose.

That a 20-year old Dylan should have turned to 'The Dæmon Lover', and in such an authentic way, as a starting point for kickstarting tradition, was surely a matter of instinct, a spark of recognition for "the only true, valid death you can feel today." But this abiding recognition of mystery as "a traditional fact" he has affirmed again and again, only recently telling Jon Pareles of the *New York Times*:

> **My songs, what makes them different is that there's a foundation to them. That's why they're still around ... They're standing on a strong foundation, and subliminally that's what people are hearing. Those old songs are my lexicon and my prayer-book.**[15]

And that house of tradition still stands. It just lies a little off the beaten path, down a narrow lane "thick beset wi' thorns and briers."

POSTSCRIPT.

The trail of weird synchronicities that tied this very strange book together continued, even as it was going to press. Two of these I'd like to share with the readers. Though I never resolved Dylan's source for the spoken introduction, the tune or arrangement of his 1961 recording, I eventually concluded that the source for his lyrics had to have been a recording by Alan Lomax of Almeda Riddle that Lomax made in early October 1959 (it was issued on CD in 1997 as Volume 6 of Rounder's Southern Journey series of Lomax recordings). Dylan would certainly have had access to the 1960 Prestige album on which this recording originally appeared, if not from Lomax, from his girlfriend's sister, Carla Rotolo, who worked for Lomax.

Though the Rounder CD contains a photo of Ms. Riddle, it is a bad reproduction. When I found a better photo of Ms. Riddle, standing with Mary Travers of Peter, Paul & Mary at Newport 1964, I realized instantly that Almeda Riddle was the very lady who is seen in Murray Lerner's Festival film suggesting that the old folksongs were probably once Pop, just before Lerner cuts to Dylan wailing out 'Maggie's Farm' at Newport 1965. I thoroughly recommend Almeda Riddle's own book of ballads, A Singer And Her Songs (Louisiana State University Press, 1970).

The other connection that, frankly, had simply not occured to me came from a review of Oh Mercy! in the L.A. Reader in September 1989, and was recently sent me by Homer the Slut. In it, one Chris Morris refers to 'Man in the Long Black Coat' as, "a chilling song-story about a diabolical stranger that takes its inspiration from centuries-old English ballads about the Demon Lover." And he is right. 'Man In The Long Black Coat' is exactly the song that would have been written by the house-carpenter when he found his wife had left with a mysterious stranger, a late twentieth-century 'James Harris'.

ACKNOWLEDGEMENTS.

This book has been more incarnations than any other work I have ever written. Though I wrote the original draft in six weeks, the editorial process has occupied some three years. My list of thanks thus begins with those who have read one or more of its drafts and given their thoughts, in particular Joel Bernstein and Andy Muir. Thanks are also due to Tony Lacey, Fran Lebowitz, David Dunton, Richard Carlin and Julian Alexander, all of whom did their best to make my efforts as publishable as possible.

I would also like to thank the staffs of the various libraries that have allowed me access to their treasures: the Houghton Library, Harvard; the Bodleian Library, Oxford; the British Library; King's College, Aberdeen; and, most especially, Malcolm Taylor and his staff at Cecil Sharp House, home of the best folksong collection in the world. Finally, I'd like to thank Rod MacBeath, David Atkinson, Greil Marcus and James Moreira for suggesting paths I might travel down; and my long-suffering girlfriend, Christine, for not glazing over everytime she heard the words demon and lover.

I'd like to dedicate what is hopefully some kind of contribution to ballad studies in the late twentieth century to its most important and perceptive exponent, the late great Professor Bertrand Bronson.

AMERICAN TEXTS THAT PRESERVE THE HILLS OF HEAVEN & HELL.

Below are the relevant verses from thity-two versions of 'House Carpenter' collected from American 'tradition' in the twentieth century to feature a dialogue between the lovers regarding the hills (or banks) of heaven and hell.

1. Bronson, B. - The Trad. Tunes of the Child Ballads.
no.20: Miss Drusilla Hall, Milford, Ala. July 23, 1952.

"What banks, what banks are those I see?
They're just as white as a snow."
"'Tis the banks of heaven," she cried unto me,
"Where all good people go."

"What banks, what banks are those I see?
They're just as black as a crow."
"'Tis the banks of hell," she cried unto me,
"Where you and I shall go."

2. Bronson, B. - The Trad. Tunes of the Child Ballads.
no.57: Robert Shiflett, Brown's Cove, Va. July 15, 1961.

"What is it that looms so dark,
As black as the feathers of a crow?"
"That is the smoke from the fires of hell,
Where you and I must go."

"What is it that looks so bright,
As white as the driven snow?"
"That is the gates of heaven itself
Where we may never go."

3. Bronson, B. - The Trad. Tunes of the Child Ballads.
no.78: Clay Walters, Salyersville, Ky. 1937.

"What hills, what hills, my own true love,
That look so white like snow?"
"It's the hills of Heaven, my own true love,
Where all righteous people go."

"What hills, what hills, my own true love,
That look so dark and low?"
"It's the hills of Hell, my own true love,
Where you and I must go."

4. Bronson, B. - The Trad. Tunes of the Child Ballads.

170

no.84: Miss Tyrah Lam, Elkton, Va. November 6, 1935.

"What hills, what hills, my false true love,
What hills so black and blue?"
"The hills you see are the hills of Hell,
Awaiting both me and you."

"What hills, what hills, my false true love,
What hills so white as snow?"
"The hills you see are the hills of Heaven,
Where you and I can't go."

5. Bronson, B. - The Trad. Tunes of the Child Ballads.
no.109b.: Mrs. Kiah Crane, Flag Pond, Tenn. October 3, 1950.

"What banks, what banks before us now,
As white as any snow?"
"It's the banks of Heaven, my love," she replied,
"Where all good people go."

"What banks, what banks before us now,
As black as any crow?"
"It's the banks of Hell, my love," she replied,
"Where you and I must go."

6. Bronson, B. - The Trad. Tunes of the Child Ballads.
no.132: Dan Tate, Fancy Gap, Va. June 1, 1962.

"What banks, what banks, my old true love?
They're as white as any snow."
"'Tis the banks of Heaven, my old true love,
Where all Christian people go."

"What banks, what banks, my old true love?
They're as black as any crow."
"'Tis the banks of Hell, my old true love,
Where both you and I must go."

7. Brown, Frank C. - North Carolina Folklore Vol.2.
Text K: Mrs. Jim Wilson, Zionville, Watauga County, NC. 1938.

"What banks are these we are passing by?
They shine like glittering gold."
"It's the banks of heaven that we are passing by,
Where you and I can't go."

"What banks are these we are landing on?
They are black as any crow."

"They are the banks of torment we are landing on
Where you and I must go."

8. Brown, Frank C. - North Carolina Folklore Vol.2.
Text M: from mss. of Phebe G.Basefield, NC. July 1940.

"Oh what white banks are that I see?
They are white as any snow."
"They are the banks of heaven, my dear,
Where your sweet little babe shall go."

"Oh what black banks are that I see?
They are blacker than any crow."
"Those are the banks of hell, my dear,
Where you and I must go."

9. Combs (ed. Wilgus) - Folk-Songs of the Southern United States.
Clarice Bailes, Clay Co., West Virginia, 1924.

"What hills are those, my own true love,
Those hills so black and blue?"
"It's the hills of hell, my own true love,
Awaiting both me and you."

"What hills are those, my own true love,
Those hills as white as snow?"
"It's the hills of heaven, my own true-love,
Where you and I can't go."

10. Cox, J.H. - Folk Songs of the South.
Text A: Mr. Decker Toney, Queens Ridge, W. Virginia, January 20, 1916.

"What hills, what hills are those, my love,
That look so bright and high?"
"It's the hills, it's the hills of heaven, my dear,
Where all righteous people lie."

"What hills, what hills, are those, my love,
That look so dark and low?"
"It's the hills, it's the hills of hell, my dear,
Where you and I must go."

11. Cox, J.H. - Folk Ballads Mainly From West Virginia.
Troy Newsome, Dingess, W. Virginia, c. 1910.

"What hills, what hills are those, my love,
That look so bright and green?"
"Those are the hills of heaven, my love,

Which you and I will never see."

"What hills, what hills are those, my love,
That look so rough and steep?"
"Those are the hills of hell, my love,
Where you and I must meet."

12. Cox, J.H. - Folk Ballads Mainly From West Virginia.
Text D: Miss Margaret Nestor, Oceana, Wyoming County, 1926.

"What hills, what hills, my own true love,
That seem so dim and high?
But oh, my old true love,
There is where all saints go when they die."

13. Davies, A.K. - Trad. Ballads of Virginia.
Text A: Mr Sam Pritt, Barber, Va. November 28, 1924.

"Oh, what is that that shines so white,
That shines as white as snow?"
"Oh those are the hills of Heaven itself,
Where we may never go."

"Oh, what is that that shines so black,
That shines as black as a crow?"
"Oh, that is the clouds of Hell itself,
Where you and I must go."

14. Davies, A.K. - Trad. Ballads of Virginia.
Text M: ??, Wise County, Va. December 1, 1916.

"O what hills, what hills, my own true love,
That looks so white like snow?"
"It is the hills of heaven where
All true lovers go."

"What hills, what hills, my own true love,
That look so black and woe?"
"It is the hills of hell, my love,
Where you and I must go."

15. Davies, A.K. - Trad. Ballads of Virginia.
Text N: ??, Wise County, Va. December 1, 1916.

"What banks, what banks, behind I see?
They are as white as any snow."
"The banks of Heaven, he cried unto her,
Where the Christian people go."

"What banks, what banks, before me I see?
They are as black as any crow."
"They are the banks of Hell, he cried unto her,
Where you and I must go."

**16. Davies, A.K. - Trad. Ballads of Virginia.
Appendix A: Mrs. Charles McAlpin, Lexington, Va. March 14, 1914.**

"See those fairy banks of heaven
White as driven snow?"
"They are the fairy banks of heaven
Where you and I can't go."

"See those cloudy banks of heaven (sic)
Dark as driven woe?"
"They are the cloudy banks of torment
Where you and I shall go."

**17. Henry, M.E. - Folk-Songs from the Southern Highlands.
Text A: Miss Ronie Johnson, Crossnore, N.C. July 1929.**

"Oh, what are the white banks that I see?
They are as white as any snow."
"They are the banks of heaven, my dear,
Where your sweet little babe shall go."

"Oh, what are the black banks that I see?
They are blacker than any crow."
"They are the banks of hell, my dear,
Where you and I must go."

**18. Henry, M.E. - Folk-Songs from the Southern Highlands.
Text C: Mrs. Hiram Proctor, Cade's Cove, Tenn, August 1928.**

"What hills, what hills, my own true love,
That look so bright above?"
"That's hills of heaven, my own true love,
Where all God's people doth go."

"What hills, what hills, my own true love,
That look so dark below?"
"That is hills of hell, my own true love,
Where you and I have started to go."

**19. Journal of American Folklore 1932.
Miss Ronie Johnson, Crossnore, Avery County, NC. July 1929.**

"Oh, what are the white banks that I see?

They are as white as any snow."
"They are the banks of heaven, my dear,
Where your sweet little babe shall go."

"Oh, what are the black banks that I see?
They are blacker than any crow."
"They are the banks of hell, my dear,
Where you and I must go."

20. McNeil, W.K. - Southern Folk Ballads Vol.2
Text A: Noble Cowden, Cushman, Arkansas, December 1979.

"What is those banks, those banks I see
That look as white as snow?
It is the banks of Heaven I know,
Where my darlin' little babe shall go." (x2)

"Oh, what is those banks, those banks I see
That looks so dark and low?
It is the banks of Hell I know,
Where you and I must go." (x2)

21. Morris, A.C. - Folksongs of Florida.
Text A: Mrs. G.A. Griffin, Newberry, Fla.

"What banks, what banks, what banks? says she,
What banks as white as snow?"
"It's banks of Heaven, a Heaven on high,
Where all good people go.[x2]"

22. Scarborough, D. - A Song Catcher in Southern Mountains.
Text D: Laura Keene, Murphy Hollow. date unknown.

"What hills, what hills, is that, my love,
That looks as white as snow?"
"That is the hills of heaven, love,
Where you and I can't go."

"What hills, what hills, is that, my love,
That looks so dark and low?"
"That is the hills of hell, my love,
Where you and I must go."

23. Scarborough, D. - A Song Catcher in Southern Mountains.
Text E: Flossie Clawson, Dark Ridge, N.C. date unknown.

"Oh, don't you see those banks, true love,
As white as any snow?

175

That's the banks of heaven, my old true love,
Where all righteous people go."

"Oh, don't you see that hole, true love,
As black as any crow?
That's the pit of hell, my old true love,
Where you and I must go."

**24. Sharp, C. - English Folk Songs from the Southern Appalachians.
Text A: Mrs. Mary Sands, Allanstand, N.C. August 1, 1916.**

"Don't you see yon light cloud arising
As light as any snow?"
That's the place called heaven, she says,
Where all righteous people go."

"Don't you see yon dark cloud arising
As dark as any crow?"
That's the place called hell, she says,
Where I and you must go."

**25. Sharp, C. - English Folk Songs from the Southern Appalachians.
Text B: Mrs. Sarah Buckner, Black Mountain, N.C. September 18, 1916.**

"What banks, what banks before us now
As white as any snow?"
"It's the banks of Heaven, my love," she replied,
Where all good people go."

"What banks, what banks before us now
As black as any crow?"
"It's the banks of hell, my love," he replied,
"Where you and I must go."

**26. Sharp, C. - English Folk Songs from the Southern Appalachians.
Text L: Miss May Ray, Harrogate, Tenn. April 29, 1917.**

"What banks, what banks is that, my love,
As black as any crow?"
"The banks, the banks of hell, my love,
Where you and I shall go."

"What banks, what banks is that, my love,
As white as any snow?"
"The banks, the banks of heaven, my love,
Where all tender little babes go."

27. Wilson, C. - Backwoods America.

176

??? collected in Eastern Tennessee.

"What hills, what hills, my own true love,
That look so bright above?"
"They're hills of heaven, my own true love,
Where all God's people go."

"What hills, what hills, my own true love,
That look so dark below?"
"That is the hills of hell, my love,
Where us two have started to go."

28. Hudson, A.P. - Folksongs of Mississippi.
Text A: Mrs. Flora Stafford Swetnam, Vaiden, Mississippi.

"Those hills, those hills, my love,
Those hills just as white as snow?"
"They are the hills of heaven, my love,
Where you and I can never go."

"Those hills, those hills, my love,
Those hills just as black as any crow?"
Those are the hills of hell, my love,
Where you and I must go."

29. Niles, J.J. - The Ballad Book.
Katherine Pettit, Lexington, Ky. Summer 1933.

"What banks, what banks of land is that, my love?
What banks so dark and so low?"
"It is the land of hell you see,
Where you and I shall go."

"What banks, what banks of land is that, my love?
What banks as white as snow?"
"It is the land of the Heavenly God
Where your sweet baby will go."

Note: Niles has almost certainly 'touched up' this published text - "banks of land" and "land of the Heavenly God" are unconvincing - though the 'dark and low - snow' lines are probably reliable.

Commercial Recordings:

30. Doug Wallin, Family Songs & Stories.
Sodom Laurel, Madison County, NC. May 23, 1983.

"Now don't you see that white cloud a-rising
As white as any snow,

177

There is a place called heaven you know
Where my tender little babe will go."

"Now don't you see that black cloud a-rising
As black as any crow
There is a place called hell you know
Where you and I must go."

31. Jean Ritchie, Folkways FA2301.

"What hills, what hills so fair and so bright,
What hills so white and fair?"
"Oh those be the hills of heaven, my dear,
But you won't never go there."

"What hills, what hills down in yonder sea,
What hills so black as coal?"
"Oh those be the hills of hell, my dear,
Where we must surely go."

32. Almeda Riddle, Prestige International INT-DS 25003.

"What are those hills, my love," she said,
"They look as white as snow."
"Those are the hills of heaven, my love,
Where your little baby will go -
But you and I will not know,
Heaven we'll never know."

"And what are those other hills," she said,
"They look as black as night,"
"Those are the hills of Hell," he said,
"Where you and I'll unite. (x2)"

BIBLIOGRAPHY:

Note: In all cases the editions cited are those I have consulted. #s of texts refers to Child Ballad 243.

(i) The Ballad Collections:
BRONSON, Bertrand - The Traditional Tunes of the Child Ballads, 4 vols. (Princeton, 1959-72) [cited as 'Bronson' - 146 texts & tunes].
CHILD, Francis J. - English & Scottish Popular Ballads, 5 vols. (Houghton-Mifflin, 1882-98) [cited as 'ESPB' - 8 texts].

ANON. - 'A Collection of Diverting Songs' (London, 1737). [1 text]
ARNOLD, Byron - Folksongs of Alabama (University of Alabama Press, 1950). ['Love Henry']
BARRY, ECKSTROM & SMYTH - British Ballads From Maine (Yale University Press, 1929). [2 texts, 1 in Bronson]
BELDEN, H.M. - Ballads & Songs (University of Missouri, 1940). [4 texts, 2 in Bronson]
BREWSTER, Paul G. - Ballads & Songs of Indiana (Indiana University Publications, 1940) [9 texts, 2 in Bronson]
BROWN, Frank C. - Collection of North Carolina Folklore, The vols. 2+4 (Duke University Press, 1952-57). [14 texts, 9 in Bronson]
BUCHAN, Peter - Ancient Ballads & Songs of the North of Scotland, 2 vols. (Edinburgh, 1828). [1 text, in Child]
BURTON, Thomas & MANNING, Ambrose - East Tennessee State University Collection of Folklore Vols. 1+2 (East Tennessee State Univ., 1967-69) [5 texts]
BUSH, Michael - Folk Songs of Central West Virginia (Custom Printing, 1969) [1 text]
CAZDEN, HAUFRECHT & STUDER - Folk Songs of the Catskills (State University of New York Press, 1982) [1 text]
CHAPPELL, Louis W. - Folk-Songs of Roanoke & the Albemarle (Ballad Press, 1939) [1 text, in Bronson]
CLAYTON, Paul - Cumberland Folksongs sleeve-notes (Folkways, 1957). [1 text]
COMBS, Josiah H. & WILGUS, D.K. - Folk-Songs of the Southern United States (University of Texas Press, 1967)
COX, John Harrington - Folk-Songs of the South (Dover Press, 1967). [5 texts, 1 in Bronson]
COX, John Harrington - Traditional Ballads Mainly From West Virginia (American Folk-Song Publications, 1939). [4 texts, 3 in Bronson]
CREIGHTON, Helen - Folksongs from Southern New Brunswick (National Museum of Canada, 1971) [1 text]
DAVIES, Arthur Kyle - Traditional Ballads of Virginia (Harvard University Press, 1929). [29 texts, 7 in Bronson]
DAVIES, Arthur Kyle - More Traditional Ballads of Virginia (Harvard University Press, 1960). [10 texts, all in Bronson]
EDDY, Mary O. - Ballads & Songs From Ohio (Folklore Associates, 1960). [5 texts, 4 in Bronson]
FLANDERS, Helen - Ancient Ballads Traditionally Sung in New England, 4 vols. (Univ. of Pennsylvania Press, 1960-65) [16 texts, 2 in Bronson]
GAINER, Patrick - Folk Songs from the West Virginia Hills (Seneca Press, 1975) [1 text]
GARDNER, E.E. & CHICKERING, G.J. - Ballads & Songs of Southern Michigan (University of Michigan Press, 1939) [3 texts, all in Bronson]
GREIG-DUNCAN Folk Song Collection, The [ed. Shuldham-Shaw & Lyle] 7 of 8 vols.

(AUP/Mercat Press 1981-1997) [1 text, in Bronson]
HENRY, Mellinger Edward - Folk-Songs From The Southern Highlands (J.J. Augustin, 1938). [4 texts, 2 in Bronson]
HUBBARD, Lester A. - Ballads and Songs from Utah (University of Utah Press, 1961) [2 texts, 1 in Bronson]
HUDSON, Arthur Palmer - Folksongs of Mississippi (University of North Carolina Press, 1936). [2 texts]
Journal of American Folklore - various.
LOMAX, Alan - Folk Songs of North America (Doubleday, 1960). [1 text]
LYLE, Emily [ed.] - Andrew Crawfurd's Collection of Songs & Ballads, 2 vols. (Scottish Text Society, 1975&96) ['The Devil's Courtship']
McNEIL, W.K. - Southern Folk Ballads Vol. 2 (August House Inc., 1988) [4 texts]
MOORE, Ethel & Chauncey O. - Ballads and Folk Songs of the Southwest (University of Oklahoma Press, 1964) [1 text]
MOORE, Arthur William - Manx Ballads and Music (1896). [1 text]
MORRIS, Alton C. - Folksongs of Florida (University of Florida Press, 1950). [2 texts, both in Bronson]
MORROW WILSON, Charles - Backwoods America (Univ. of North Carolina Press, 1934). [1 text]
MOTHERWELL, William - Minstrelsy: Ancient and Modern (Glasgow, 1827). [1 text, in Child]
NILES, John Jacob - The Ballad Book of... (Houghton Mifflin, 1961). [1 text, in Child]
ORD, John - The Bothy Songs & Ballads (John Donald, 1995). ['Sir John Gordon']
OWENS, William A. - Texas Folk Songs (Texas Folklore Society, 1950). [1 text, in Bronson]
PEACOCK, Kenneth - Songs of the Newfoundland Outports Vol. 3 (National Museum of Canada, 1965) [1 text]
PERCY, Bishop - Reliques of Ancient English Poetry (J. Dodsley, 1775).
POUND, Louise - American Ballads and Songs (Charles Scribner's, 1972) [1 text]
RAINEY, Leo - Songs of the Ozark Folk (The Ozarks Mountaineer, 1976) [1 text qv. McNeil]
RANDOLPH, Vance - Ozark Folksongs Vol.1 ((University of Missouri Press, 1980) [16 texts, 8 in Bronson]
SANDBURG, Carl - The American Songbag (Harcourt, Brace & Co., 1927). [1 text, in Bronson]
SCARBOROUGH, Dorothy - Song Catcher in the Southern Mountains (Columbia University Press, 1937) [6 texts, 3 in Bronson]
SCOTT, Sir Walter [ed. Henderson, T.F.] - Minstrelsy of the Scottish Border (Oliver & Boyd, 1932). [1 text, in Child]
SHARP, Cecil - English Folk Songs From The Southern Appalachians 2 vols. (Oxford University Press, 1932) [22 texts, all in Bronson]
SHELLANS, Herbert - Folk Songs of the Blue Ridge Mountains (Oak Publications, 1968) [1 text]
SMITH, Reed - South Carolina Ballads (Harvard University Press, 1928) [2 texts]
STOUT, Earl J. - Folklore from Iowa (American Folklore Society, 1936) [2 texts]
WARNER, Anne - Traditional American Folk Songs (Syracuse University Press, 1984) [1 text]
WILLIAMS, Alfred - Folk Songs of the Upper Thames (Duckworth & Co., 1923). ['A Riddle Wisely Expounded']

(ii) Manuscript sources:
BUCHAN, Peter - Secret Songs of Silence ms. (Harvard Univ.)
BUCHAN, Peter - British Museum ms. (British Museum)
BUCHAN-MOTHERWELL correspondence. (Harvard Univ.)

CARPENTER, James ms. (Cecil Sharp House)
MOTHERWELL, William - ballad ms. (Harvard Univ.)
MOTHERWELL, William - Ballad notebook 1826-27. (Harvard Univ.)
SCOTT, Robert - Glenbuchat ms. (King's College, Aberdeen)

(iii) Commentary, Historical and Bibliographical sources:
ANON. - The Complaynt of Scotland (Scottish Text Society, 1993)
ANDERSEN, Fleming - Commonplace & Creativity (Odense University Press, 1985)
ATKINSON, David - "Marriage & Retribution in 'James Harris'" in Folk Music Journal vol.5 no.5, 1989.
AYTOUN, William E. - The Ballads of Scotland, 2 vols.(Blackwood & Sons, 1858)
BARING-GOULD, Sabine - Songs of the West (Metheun & Co., 1905).
BARING-GOULD, Sabine - An Historical Sketch of English National Song (Acorn, 1895)
BRONSON, Bertrand - The Ballad As Song (Univ. of California, 1969).
BUCHAN, David - 'The Maid, the Palmer, and the Cruel Mother' in The Malahat Review 1967.
BUCHAN, David - The Ballad and the Folk (Tuckwell Press, 1997).
BURRISON, John - "'James Harris' in Britain since Child" in Journal of American Folklore 80:317
CHAMBERS, E.K. - English Literature at the Close of the Middle Ages (Oxford, 1945).
CHAMBERS, Robert - Popular Rhymes of Scotland (Edinburgh, 1870).
CHAPPELL, William - Old English Popular Music (Jack Brussel, 1961).
CHARTERS, Samuel - The Poetry of the Blues (Oak Publications, 1963).
CHAUCER, Geoffrey [ed. Nevill Coghill] - The Canterbury Tales (Penguin Classics, 1951)
CHEESMAN, Tom & RIEUWERTS, Sigrid [ed.] - Ballads Into Books (Peter Long, 1997).
CHILD, Francis J. - The Scholar-Friends (Greenwood Press, 1970).
CLAWSON, W.H. - The Geste of Robin Hood (University of Toronto Press, 1909).
COFFIN, Tristram - The British Traditional Ballad in North America (American Folklore Soc., 1950).
DEAN-SMITH, Margaret - A Guide to English Folk Song Collections 1822-1952 (University Press of Liverpool, 1954).
DUGAW, Dianne - The Anglo-American Ballad: A Folklore Casebook (Garland Publishing, 1995).
DUNCAN, Edmondstoune - The Story of Minstrelsy (Walter Scott Publishing Co., 1907)
DUNCAN, J.B. - Folk Song in the North East [lecture]
DYLAN, Bob - Lyrics (Knopf, 1985)
FISCHER, David Hackett - Albion's Seed (Oxford University Press, 1989).
FOWLER, David C. - A Literary History of the Popular Ballad (Duke University Press, 1968).
FRIEDMAN, Albert B. - The Viking Book of Ballads of the English-Speaking World (Viking Press, 1956).
FRIEDMAN, Albert B. - article in Essays Presented to Bertrand Bronson [ed. James Porter] (Univ. of California, 1983).
FURNIVALL, Frederick J. - Captain Cox, his Ballads & Books (The Ballad Society, 1871).
FURNIVALL, Frederick J. & John W. Hales - The Percy Folio (The Early English Text Society, 1867-68).
GEROULD, Gordon Hall - The Ballad of Tradition (Gordian Press, 1974).
GOLDSTEIN, Ken - transcript of interview with James Carpenter.
GRAVES, Robert - The English Ballad (Ernest Benn Ltd., 1927).
GRAVES, Robert - [English & Scottish] Ballads (Heinemann, 1957).
GRAVES, Robert - Goodbye To All That (Jonathan Cape, 1930).
GREENWAY, John - American Folksongs of Protest (Philadelphia, 1953)

HARKER, Dave - 'The Price You Pay' in Lost in Music [ed. Avron Levine White (Routledge and Kegan Paul, 1987).

HARKER, Dave - Fakesong: The Manufacture of British 'Folksong' 1700 to the Present Day (Open University, 1985).

HECHT, Hans - 'Thomas Percy und William Shenstone, ein Briefwechsel' in Quellen und Forschungen, 1909.

HENDERSON, T.F. - The Ballad in Literature (Cambridge University Press, 1912).

HODGART, M.J.C. - The Ballads (Hutchinson University Library, 1950)

HUMPHRIES, Patrick - Richard Thompson: Strange Affair (Virgin, 1996).

HUSTVEDT, Sigurd Bernhard - Ballad Books & Ballad Men (Harvard, 1930).

IVES, Edward D. - The Bonnie Earl of Murray (University of Illinois, 1997).

KARPELES, Maud - Folk Songs from Newfoundland (Faber, 1971).

KEITH, Alexander & GREIG, Gavin - Last Leaves of Traditional Ballads & Ballad Airs (Aberdeen, 1925).

KITTREDGE, George Lyman [ed.] - Child's English & Scottish Popular Ballads [Cambridge Edition] (Houghton-Mifflin, 1904).

LAWLESS, Ray M. - Folksingers & Folksongs in America (Duell, Sloan & Pearce, 1960).

LAWS, G. Malcolm - American Balladry from British Broadsides (PAFS, 1957).

LAWS, G. Malcolm - Native American Balladry (PAFS, 1950).

LEACH, MacEdward - The Ballad Book (A.S. Barnes & Co., 1955).

LLOYD, A.L. - Folk Songs in England (International Publishers, 1967).

MacKAY, Julie Reich - Medieval Metrical Saints' Lives (PhD thesis, Univ. of Penn., 1968)

MacNUTT, W.S. - The Atlantic Provinces: The Emergence of Colonial Society (McClelland & Stewart, 1965).

MARCUS, Greil - Invisible Republic (Henry Holt, 1997).

McCONCHEY, James [ed.] - The Poetical Works of William Motherwell (David Robertson, 1847).

McGREGOR, Craig - Bob Dylan: A Retrospective (Morrow, 1971).

McKENZIE, W. Roy - The Quest of the Ballad (Princeton, 1919).

MELLERS, Wilfred - Darker Shade of Pale: A Backdrop to Bob Dylan (Faber & Faber, 1984)

MONTGOMERIE, William - A Bibliography of Scottish Ballad Manuscripts 1730-1825 in Studies in Scottish Literature Parts I-V [1966-69].

OLSON, Ian - Editing the Glenbuchat ballads in The Aberdeen University Review Spring 1997.

PALMER, Roy - 'Veritable Dunghills: Professor Child and the Ballad' in Folk Music Journal Vol.7 No.2.

PARRY, Milman - 'Studies in the Epic Technique of Oral Verse-Making' in Harvard Studies in Classical Philology 1930 & 1932.

PATTERSON, B.& D. - sleeve-notes to Smithsonian CD SF 40013.

POUND, Louise - Poetic Origins and The Ballad (New York, 1921).

QUILLER-COUCH, Sir Arthur - The Oxford Book of Ballads (Oxford University Press, 1910)

RICHMOND, W. Edson - Ballad Scholarship: An Annotated Bibliography (Garland, 1989).

RIMBAULT, Edward F. - Musical Illustrations of Bishop Percy's Reliques (London, 1850).

RITSON, Joseph - A Select Collection of English Songs (London, 1813).

SHAKESPEARE, William - The Complete Works [ed. Wells & Taylor] (Oxford University Press, 1988).

SHARP, Cecil - English Folk Song: Some Conclusions (Metheun, 1907).

SPENCE, Lewis - The Magic Arts in Celtic Britain (Constable, 1995).

STEENSTRUP, Johannes - [translated E.G. Cox] The Medieval Popular Ballad (Univ. of Washington Press, 1968).

TOLKEIN, J.R.R.[ed.] - Sir Gawain, Pearl, Sir Orfeo (Houghton-Mifflin, 1975).
TOSCHES, Nick - Country (Secker & Warburg, 1989).
WWALKER, William - Peter Buchan & Other Papers (D. Wyllie & Son, 1915).
WILGUS, D.K. - Anglo-American Folksong Scholarship (Rutgers University Press, 1959).
WIMBERLY, Lowry Charles - Folklore in the English & Scottish Ballads (Univ. of Chicago Press, 1928).

(iv) Journals:
Journal of American Folklore 1888-present.
Journal of the Folk-Song Society 1899-1931.
Journal of the English Folk-Dance and Song Society 1932-1963.
Folk Music Journal 1965-present.
Southern Folklore Quarterly 1937-present.

SELECTED RECORDINGS OF 'THE HOUSE CARPENTER' -

ASHLEY, Clarence - Anthology of American Folk Music Vol. 1 (Folkways FA 2951)
BORUSKY, Pearl Jacobs - Child Ballads Traditional In The U.S. Vol. 2 (Library of Congress AFS L58).
CLAYTON, Paul - CUMBERLAND FOLKSONGS (Folkways FA 2007).
DYER-BENNETT, Richard - Songs (DYB 3000).
DYLAN, Bob - The Bootleg Series (Columbia CK 47399).
GLADDEN, Texas - Anglo-American Ballads (Library of Congress AFS L1).
KINCAID, Bradley - Favourite Ballads and Old Time Songs (Old Homestead OHCS 155).
OGAN GUNNING, Sarah - The Silver Dagger (Rounder 0051).
RIDDLE, Almeda - Songs and Ballads of the Ozarks (Vanguard VRS 9158).
RITCHIE, Jean - British Traditional Ballads In The Southern Mountains Vol.1 (Folkways FA 2301).
SEEGER, Peggy - Folk Songs of Courting and Complaint (Folkways FP 49).
STEELE, Pete - Banjo Tunes and Songs (Folkways FS 3828)
VAN RONK, Dave - Blues In The Bottle (Big Beat CDWIK 71).
WALLIN, Doug - Family Songs & Stories From The North Carolina Mountains (Smithsonian-Folkways CD 40013).
WALTERS, Clay - Child Ballads Traditional In The U.S. Vol. 2 (Library of Congress AFS L58).
WEST, Hedy - Pretty Saro & Other Appalachian Ballads (Topic 12T146).

NOTES:

Preface -
(1) McGregor ed. p130.
(2) transcribed from THE BOOTLEG SERIES (Sony C3K 47382).
(3) Lawless p65.
(4) JAF 1917 pp207-9.
(5) CUMBERLAND FOLKSONGS insert.
(6) transcribed from BLUES IN THE BOTTLE (Big Beat CDWIK 71).
(7) Lawless p128.
(8) Scott I, pp6-7.

Chapter 1 -
(1) Harker p107.
(2) Tosches pp19-20.
(3) Chappell p9.
(4) Dugaw ed. p5.
(5) Bronson - The Ballad As Song ppp75-6.
(6) Graves - Ballads p149.
(7) Child IV, p362.
(8) Scott III, 246.
(9) Dugaw ed. pp58-59.
(10) ibid. p62.
(11) Graves - English Ballad p8.
(12) Hecht p54-55.
(13) Graves - English Ballad p9.
(14) Leach p3.
(15) Dugaw pp48-9.
(16) Graves - English Ballad p32.
(17) Percy p xii.
(18) Ritson p xii-xiii.
(19) Hustvedt p206.
(20) Greig pp7-8,11.
(21) Humphries p82.
(22) Child - The Scholar-Friend pp44-45.
(23) transcribed from Westwood Radio Show 1985.
(24) ESPB I, p324

Chapter 2 -:
(1) Hustvedt p254.
(2) 'A Collection of Diverting Songs' pp466-67.
(3) JAF 1917 pp207-9.
(4) ESPB IV, p365.
(5) ESPB IV, p365.
(6) ESPB IV, p366.
(7) ibid.
(8) Graves - Ballads p149.
(9) Andersen p74-75.
(10) Gerould p257.
(11) Bronson III p464.
(12) ibid. III p464.
(13) ibid. III p464.
(14) ESPB IV, pp365-66.
(15) Bronson III, p466.
(16) ibid. III, p467.
(17) ibid. III p466.

Chapter 3 -:
(1) Euing Collection pp628-29.
(2) Morrow Wilson pp96-7.
(3) Atkinson pp602/4.
(4) Flanders III, p318.
(5) ibid. III, pp318-19.
(6) Chambers 20th Century Dictionary.
(7) Flanders III, p319.
(8) Bronson III, p466.
(9) Flanders III, p319.
(10) Lomax p170.
(11) ESPB IV, p361.
(12) ibid. IV, pp362-64.
(13) Harker pp107-63.
(14) Baring-Gould Chapter - p22.
(15) Graves - Ballads p149.
(16) ESPB IV, p361.
(17) More Davies p271.
(18) ESPB IV, pp362-64.
(19) ibid IV, 364.
(20) ibid III, 208.
(21) DNB [1967-8], XVI , p333..
(22) Harker pp107-63.
(23) Harker pp107-63.
(24) ESPB III, p208.
(25) ibid. II, p430.
(26) ibid. II, p429.
(27) Bronson II, p530.
(28) ibid. II, p530.
(29) ibid. II, p530.
(30) Atkinson p600.
(31) ibid. p600.
(32) ESPB IV, p364.
(33) Moore p119.
(34) Aytoun II, p3.
(35) Buchan, Peter I, p313.

Chapter 4 -:
(1) Notes & Queries July 14, 1855.
(2) qv. Buchan, David p212.
(3) Walker p49.
(4) Hustvedt p248.
(5) ibid. pp249-50.
(6) ibid. p264.

(7) ESPB IV, p435.
(8) Walker p--
(9) letter to William Motherwell, July 31, 1826.
(10) letter to William Motherwell, April 1827.
(11) ESPB IV, pp364-66
(12) Greig-Duncan II p490.

Chapter 5 -:
(1) Duncan p11.
(2) ESPB IV, p364.
(3) ibid. IV, p365.
(4) ibid. IV, p363.
(5) ibid. IV, p365.
(6) ibid. IV, p365.
(7) ibid. IV, p363.
(8) ibid. IV, p366.
(9) ibid. IV, p364
(10) ibid. IV, p390
(11) Bronson IV, p15.
(12) Bronson IV, p21.
(13) Bronson IV, p15.
(14) Bronson IV, p15.
(15) ESPB II, p230.
(16) Bronson II, p229.
(17) ibid. II, p231.
(18) ibid. II, p229.
(19) Parry 1932, p7.
(20) Parry 1930, p80.
(21) Friedman - Essays p231.
(22) Andersen p286.
(23) Andersen p32.
(24) Child II, p233.
(25) ibid. IV, p366.
(26) Wimberley p--
(27) ESPB I, p232.

Chapter 6 -:
(1) Child - The Scholar-Friend p56.
(2) Hustvedt p296.
(3) ibid.
(4) Studies in Scottish Lit. V, p108.
(5) Aberdeen University Review Spring 1997, p35.
(6) Malahat Review 1967 pp100-1.
(7) ibid. p100.
(8) ESPB IV, p430
(9) ESPB IV, p434.
(10) Bronson - The Ballad As Song p145.
(11) text provided by Dr. Jamie Moreira.
(12) ESPB II, p318.

Chapter 7 -:
(1) ESPB IV, p369.
(2) ESPB IV, p368.
(3) ibid. IV, p368.
(4) Flanders III, pp315-16.
(5) Flanders III, p316.
(6) ESPB IV, p366.
(7) ESPB IV, p369.
(8) Scott I, p x.

(9) Child IV, p369..
(10) Scott II, p55.
(11) McConechy p xxxiii.
(12) Motherwell pp93-94.
(13) ESPB IV, pp367-68.
(14) ibid. IV, p368.
(15) Cheesman [ed.] p--.

Chapter 8 -:
(1) ESPB IV, p362.
(2) Dugaw ed. p61.
(3) ESPB I, p3.
(4) ibid. I, p5.
(5) ibid. I, p3.
(6) ibid. I, p4.
(7) ibid. V, p284.
(8) Williams p37.
(9) ESPB II, 29.
(10) ESPB IV, p454.
(11) Andersen p102.
(12) Lyle ed. xvi.
(13) Graves - Ballads p147.
(14) Lyle ed. pp104-5.
(15) Lyle ed. p105.
(16) Chambers - Popular Rhymes p62.
(17) Chambers - Popular Rhymes p61.
(18) Greig-Duncan IV, p229.
(19) Gerould p139.

Chapter 9 -:
(1) Fischer p605.
(2) ibid. pp785-86.
(3) Annals of Philadelphia qv. Fischer.
(4) ibid. pp606 + 621-22.
(5) ibid. pp633-34.
(6) McIntyre p17.
(7) MacNutt p62.
(8) Karpeles p17.
(9) MacKenzie p124.
(10) Davies p441 [Version a]
(11) Davies p197 [version c]
(12) ESPB IV, p365.
(13) Harker pp 138.
(14) Burrison p277.
(15) ESPB IV, p367.
(16) ibid. IV, p68 [Child 200D].
(17) Davies p441.
(18) Bronson IV, p508.

Chapter 10 -:
(1) Journal des Savants, July 1898.
(2) Bronson IV, p508.
(3) ESPB III, p42.
(4) Scott IV, p81.
(5) ESPB I, p317.
(6) Scott IV, pp82-83.
(7) ESPB I, p318.
(8) Tolkein p123
(9) Duncan p79

(10) ESPB I, p318
(11) ESPB I, p319.
(12) Scott IV, p95
(13) ESPB I, pp324.
(14) Davies p476.
(15) Henderson p10
(16) ESPB IV, p454.
(17) ESPB I p257.
(18) ibid. I, p336.
(19) ibid. I, p336.
(20) ESPB I, pp343-35.
(21) ibid. I, p342.
(22 Scott II, p379.
(23) Studies in Scottish Lit. VI, p91-104.
(24) ESPB IV, p455.
(25) Scott IV, p96.
(26) Child I, p328.
(27) Ord p423
(28) Graves - Ballads p148.
(29) ESPB I, p345.
(30) Ord p425.
(31) Graves - Ballads p147.
(32) Spence p65.
(33) ESPB IV, p458.
(34) qv. Buchan, D. p214.
(35) Bronson I, p10.
(36) Bronson - The Ballad As Song p145.

Chapter 11 -:
(1) Chambers, R.K. p169.
(2) Gerould pp2-3.
(3) Duncan p145.
(4) Shakespeare p700.
(5) Bronson I, p138.
(6) ESPB I, p114.
(7) Bronson I, 138.
(8) Diary of Issac Walton.
(9) qv. Baring-Gould - English National Song p6.
(10) Fowler p102.
(11) Lomax p170.
(12) Steenstrup p7.
(13) Williams p9.
(14) Williams pp19-20.
(15) letter to William Motherwell, January 17, 1826.
(16) letter to William Motherwell, April 1827.
(17) letter to William Motherwell, July 31, 1826.
(18) Friedman p ix.
(19) Motherwell's notebook.
(20) Bronson - The Ballad As Song pp72-73.
(21) Buchan, David p76.
(22) transcript of interview by K. Goldstein.

Chapter 12 -:
(1) Graves - The English Ballad p18.
(2) Bronson - The Ballad As Song p61.
(3) Kittredge p xiii.
(4) Bronson - The Ballad As Song p61.
(5) ibid. pp74-75.
(6) ibid. p61.

(7) ibid.
(8) ibid. pp118-19.
(9) Buchan, D. p235.
(10) Buchan, D. p--.
(11) Buchan, D. pp235-36.
(12) Buchan, D. p242.
(13) Bronson III, pp494-95.
(14) Burrison p283.
(15) Gerould p180
(16) Hustvedt p229
(17) Sharp p31.
(18) Coffin pp17-18
(19) Lloyd p140.
(20) Sandburg p66.
(21) Lomax pp169-70.
(22) Marcus p179.
(23) Hodgart p35
(24) Buchan, David p171.
(25) 'Family Songs & Stories' (Smithsonian SF 40013)

Chapter 13 -:
(1) qv. Mellers p33.
(2) Shakespeare p662.
(3) ibid. p669.
(4) ibid. p1120.
(5) Friedman pp54-55.
(6) Bronson - The Ballad As Song p61.
(7) Lloyd pp 139-40.
(8) Mellers p44.
(9) Stearns p14.
(10) Charters p9.
(11) Sackheim, p224.
(12) Marcus p195.
(13) Scott I, p x.
(14) Graves - Goodbye To All That p26.
(15) The Daily Telegraph October 5, 1997.

Available From Helter Skelter Publishing

Bob Dylan by Anthony Scaduto 1-900924-00-5 £11.95
The first and best biography of Dylan.

"Scaduto's 1971 book was the pioneering portrait of this legendarily elusive artist. Now in a welcome reprint it's a real treat to read the still-classic Bobography".
Paul Du Noyer, Q***

"Superb on the Greenwich Village scene, insightful on the meaning of John Wesley Harding ... it's still perhaps the best book ever written on Dylan".

Solo: A Biography of Sandy Denny by Pamela Winters
Due in May. 256 pages,   ISBN 1 900924 11 0   Price: £12.99
Sandy Denny became famous as the distinctive singer Fairport Convention, and later with Fotheringay, as well as releasing four highly acclaimed solo albums. Melody Maker voted her best female singer in 1970 and 1971. But like many of the great musical artists of the seventies, she took refuge in drink and drugs. Sandy Denny died 20 years ago in mysterious circumstances, and this is the first ever Biography. US music journalist Pam Winters has had unprecedented access to Sandy's personal papers. She has interviewed at length all those who were close to her, to produce an illuminating portrait of one of the great English

Back To The Beach - A Brian Wilson and the Beach Boys Reader
edited by Kingley Abbott 1-900924-02-1 £12.99
A collection of the best articles about Brian and the band, together with a number of previously unpublished pieces and some specially commissioned work. Features Nick Kent, David Leaf, Timothy White and others with a foreword by Brian.
"A detailed study and comprehensive overview of the BB's lives and music. Most impressively Abbott manages to appeal to both die-hard fans and rather less obsessive newcomers." **Time Out**
"Rivetting!" **** Q Magazine**

Born In The USA - Bruce Springsteen and the American Tradition
by Jim Cullen 1-900924-05-6 £9.99

The first major study of Bruce Springsteen's that looks at his music in the context of his blue collar roots, and his place in American culture

"Cullen has written an excellent treatise expressing exactly how and why Springsteen translated his uneducated hicktown American-ness into music and stories that touched hearts and souls all around the world." **Q****
"This is a provocative look at one of America's cultural icons." **Newsweek**

Available From Helter Skelter Publishing

Like The Night -
Bob Dylan and the Road to the Manchester Free Trade Hall.
ISBN: 1 900924 07 2   192 pages (illustrated). UK £12.00
The full history and background to the show that would become Bob Dylan's latest album, the most famous bootleg in history, now The Bootleg Series vols 4 and 5.
"When Dylan went electric, he both alienated the audience that had championed him and changed the face of rock music.
Lee's enjoyable and atmospheric reconstruction of this phase of Dylan's career is essential reading.' **Uncut Magazine**

Waiting for the Man: The Story of Drugs and Popular Music
by Harry Shapiro
Due in April 320 pages, ISBN 1 900924 08 0   Price: £12.99
First published in 1988, this is the definitive study of the extravagant, if sombre, association between drugs and popular music. Shapiro tells in detail the stories of the most famous heroes - Charlie Parker, Jimi Hendrix, Jim Morrison, Keith Moon, Sid Vicious - and examines the relationship between two billion-dollar industries. Fully revised, and including over 100 pages of new material covering the rise of Ecstasy and dance music; rap music and "crack" cocaine, and the return of the wasted junky rock star that came with the Seattle grunge scene. Featured artists in these new sections include Shaun Ryder, Tupac Shakur and Kurt Cobain.

GET BACK: The Beatles' Let It Be Disaster
by Doug Sulphy and Ray Schweighhardt
ISBN: 1 900924 12 9   256 pages   UK £12.99
A detailed document of the group's breakdown seen through the prism of the Get Back recording sessions. Instead of making the planned new album, the greatest band in the world were falling apart.
"One of the most poignant Beatles books ever." **Patrick Humphries, MOJO**
"Monumental... Fascinating and revealing" **Goldmine**

All Helter Skelter titles can be ordered direct from the world famous
Helter Skelter music bookstore which is situated at:

Helter Skelter,
4 Denmark Street, London WC2H 8LL
Tel: +44 (0) 171 836 1151   Fax: +44 (0) 171 240 9880.
Consult our website at: http://www.skelter.demon.co.uk

This store has the largest collection of music books anywhere in the world and can supply any in-print title by mail to any part of the globe. For a mail order catalogue or for wholesaling enquiries, please contact us.